Contents

Introduction

Welcome to our guide for the CSLB Contractor's License Exam. If you have ever felt overwhelmed by the dense and comprehensive California code books, you are not alone. That's precisely why we created this guide: to distill the vast and intricate content of those code books into a format that's not only digestible but also easy to retain.

We recognize the importance of aligning our material with the CSLB's guidelines. To that end, we've organized the contents of this guide to mirror the seven main sections as laid out in the CSLB Law and Business study guide. We've also included an additional section related to topics you would see in the General Building (B) exam. At the end of each section, there is a series of questions designed to help reinforce the concepts that were covered, ensuring that you grasp each topic thoroughly. Whether you are a seasoned professional looking for a quick refresher or a newcomer aiming to understand the basics, we believe this guide will serve as an invaluable resource in your preparation.

Remember, while we have done our utmost to ensure accuracy and relevance, it is always a good idea to cross-reference with the latest editions of the California code books, as codes and regulations can evolve over time.

We wish you the best of luck in your upcoming exam. Dive in, and let's embark on this journey of mastering the essentials of the California Contractor's License Exam together!

Lastly, your success is our benchmark. Every review helps us refine our approach, benefiting countless test takers. Start your preparation with confidence, and once you feel the impact, please help us grow with your feedback. Positive reviews from wonderful test takers like you help other test takers feel confident about choosing test prep materials like this resource. Sharing your experience will be appreciated! Happy studying!

Business Organization and Licensing

Project Management

Project management plays a pivotal role in determining the success of a construction project. It is a complex task that demands a blend of managerial skills and a comprehensive understanding of the design and construction process. A project manager (PM) is responsible for managing the project timeline through effective scheduling, considering factors such as budget constraints, quality standards, resource management, and planning specifications.

The project manager serves as the primary contact for the owner and could either be the owner of the company or an employee of the construction management company. The PM possesses the necessary knowledge and skills to oversee various stages of construction, gained through firsthand experience. However, the key to successful project management lies in the ability to analyze available information and make informed decisions.

Project management involves coordinating workers and materials to see a project through to completion. Management theory can be divided into two areas: functional and behavioral. Functional management pertains to the technical business aspects such as planning, budgeting, and schedule preparation. It involves good planning to keep resources available, delegating tasks, standardizing operations for optimal efficiency, and organizing job task records to monitor progress and identify potential issues.

Behavioral management, on the other hand, deals with the personnel side of the business. A construction project manager works closely with the project superintendent and the workers to ensure smooth site activity. This involves proper treatment of personnel, fostering cooperation, delegating responsibility and authority, and maintaining clear communication. As the business grows, the contractor must spend more time in the managerial role, focusing on exceptions to normal operation.

Project supervisors and managers may be required depending on the project size. The supervisory team works with the project manager to oversee the daily aspects of the project. A superintendent supervises the daily on-site operations and progress, ensuring the project is completed on time and within budget. A foreman, who reports to the superintendent, is responsible for supervising specific trade areas, estimating the materials, equipment, and supplies needed for routine work, and assigning a crew as needed.

In a construction project, all phases must be coordinated to minimize wasted time and complete the project as soon as possible. This involves reviewing the bid, dividing the project into segments, scheduling all phases of the project, making a list of items that must be pre-ordered, and identifying potential problems.

Contractors can use three basic scheduling systems: the calendar planner, the bar chart (or Gantt chart), and the critical path method (CPM). The calendar planner is the simplest method, suitable for small jobs and businesses. The bar chart uses a linear grid to show the relationship between all phases and display which phases exceeded the estimated time. The CPM, though complex, is the most effective method. It uses a diagram to divide a project into its component parts and shows the order of task sequences. The critical path is the one with the longest completion time, and any delays in this path will delay the entire project.

Understanding Business Structures

This chapter focuses on the business organization aspect of the Contractors State License Board (CSLB) exam. It is designed to help you understand the law and business portion of the test, with each chapter corresponding to a specific section of the exam. The topics covered include business organization, business finances, employment requirements, bonds, insurance and liens, contracts, licensing, safety, and public works.

The average contractor possesses a wealth of knowledge and skills acquired from hands-on experience in various construction phases. However, a contractor must also be adept at planning and managing a business, coordinating employee work, materials, and training, and providing guidance to both supervisory and non-supervisory employees. This chapter will delve into the skills and guidelines necessary for effective business and worker management.

A business organization is a collective term used to describe a group of individuals with a specific purpose and structure. It is an entity created for professional, commercial, and industrial activities. Some business organizations are profit-oriented, designed to generate income for their owners, while others are nonprofit organizations serving public purposes.

A business plan is a crucial component of a business, outlining the strategy for success and providing a roadmap for the business's growth. It serves as a benchmark detailing the company's financial status and outlines both the operational and financial objectives for the future, along with strategies to achieve these objectives. It also highlights potential problems and their solutions, describes the business's organizational structure, and specifies the required capital. A business plan is typically required when seeking investment or a loan.

Before starting a business, one of the first steps is to decide on the firm's legal structure. This decision will determine the availability of financing, individual liability, and control. The transformation from one form of business to another is considered a growth process. For instance, a sole proprietor may form a partnership or a corporation to gain additional financial resources.

Each business structure has its advantages and disadvantages. The following sections provide examples of the various business options available to an individual business owner.

1. **Individual or Sole Proprietorship**: This is a business form where an individual owns all of the business's equity and is solely responsible for debts and liabilities incurred by the business. It is the simplest and easiest form of business to establish, requiring minimum regulations. However, the owner is personally responsible for all financing, and the business dissolves once the owner passes away.
2. **Partnership**: A partnership is created when the ownership and management of a business are shared by two or more individuals. The rights and responsibilities of the partners regarding profit and loss sharing and other business-related activities are identified in the partnership agreement. A partnership business may be general or limited. In a general partnership, each partner is liable to the extent of their personal assets. In a limited partnership, the partners do not hold full business responsibility and are liable up to the extent of their original investment.
3. **C Corporation**: A C Corporation is a separate legal entity that can consist of one or more individuals. To qualify as a corporation, individuals must file articles of incorporation with the Secretary of State. A C Corporation includes a governing body of officers and is owned by one or more shareholders. It is legally liable for its operations, and its earnings are separately taxed. A C Corporation does not terminate upon the death of one or more shareholders or the sale of stocks. Double taxation is an inevitable aspect of business, where taxes are imposed on both business

profits and individual dividends. Establishing a complex structure is more costly and comes with more legal requirements, including strict rules and regulations that govern startup and operations. Unlike S corporations, there is no advantage of deducting corporate losses.

4. **S corporation**: S corporations have unique tax considerations that differ from those of C corporations. They are not subject to double taxation. However, S corporation status is only available if the corporation is domestically held, has one class of stock, and only allows individuals, certain trusts, and estates to become shareholders. The business income of an S corporation is reported as individual income, even though it operates in a corporate form. This limits the owner's liability and taxes it in the same way as a partnership. An S corporation may not have more than 100 shareholders, and all shareholders must consent to the S corporation status. S corporations are often more appealing to small business owners than C corporations due to their advantages. These include limited liability protection for shareholders and management, pass-through taxation for its members (similar to a partnership), and perpetual existence. However, S corporations are subject to yearly tax filing requirements. Some disadvantages include the restriction to domestic capital, a maximum of 100 shareholders, and closer scrutiny from the IRS due to complex tax qualification requirements.

5. **Limited Liability Company**: A Limited Liability Company (LLC) is a corporate structure where members (owners) are not personally liable for the organization's debts and liabilities. They benefit from limited liability protection, but this does not extend to personal actions. An LLC has many of the same legal protections as a C corporation, but it is not subject to double taxation. Federal taxes are paid on profit income distributed to members. An LLC requires less paperwork and regulation than C corporations. Advantages of an LLC include less public exposure of members, fewer paperwork and documentation requirements, and no public disclosure of financial reports. LLCs also offer limited liability for managers and members, and no taxation at the entity level. However, owners of an LLC must immediately recognize profits, if any, and an LLC offers fewer fringe benefits for owners and management. If a member leaves the LLC, the LLC typically dissolves. Profits of an LLC are taxed with Medicare and Social Security.
    a. Additional requirements for an LLC license include a $100,000 surety bond, in addition to the required contractor bond, should the LLC fail to pay wages. Every member of the LLC, including officers, responsible managers, or directors, must be listed as personnel of record. Liability insurance with an aggregate limit of $1 million is required for a licensed LLC with five or fewer members. An additional $100,000 is required for every additional personnel of record, up to $5 million total. An LLC may serve as a partner on a partnership license or as part of a joint venture. Most of the requirements and provisions that apply to corporate licenses also apply to an LLC.

6. **Joint Venture**: A joint venture occurs when two or more organizations collaborate on a specific project. These companies share returns, risks, and governance in a new entity, which may be managed as a corporation, LLC, or partnership. A joint venture license application is submitted by two or more separate licensees wanting to act together on contract work. An exam or qualifying individual is not required to obtain this kind of license, as only currently licensed businesses are permitted to be involved. Separate businesses may act together under this type of license, which must be renewed every two years, the same as a standard contractor's license. For more information on the advantages and disadvantages of business structures, please refer to the law and business manual.

Navigating Construction Permits, Certifications, and Registrations in California

In California, particularly for those preparing for the CSLB contractor's license exam, understanding the permit, registration, and certification requirements is essential. Here's a breakdown to make this clearer:

Cal OSHA Construction Permits:

Cal OSHA oversees construction activity permits for several specific tasks:

1. Trenches or excavations 5 feet or deeper that require personal entry.

2. Constructing, tearing down, or dismantling buildings, scaffolding, or other structures more than three stories or 36 feet high.

3. Setting up or taking down vertical shoring systems exceeding three stories or the equivalent height.

To secure a permit, contractors must:

- Schedule a safety permit conference at the nearest Cal OSHA district office.

- The attendee, usually the contractor, should be knowledgeable about the specific activity.

- Discuss potential health and safety risks and the steps to counteract them.

- Review the details against Title 8 safety orders pertinent to the task.

To verify the safety of the proposed task, contractors should provide:

- A filled-out permit application.

- An activity notification form.

- The contractor's Injury and Illness Prevention (IIP) program.

- The contractor's safety practices code.

Tower Crane Requirements:

For both stationary and mobile tower cranes:

- A special tower crane permit is essential.

- Reach out to the nearest crane unit to process the permit application and arrange inspections.

- If operating cranes with a capacity surpassing three tons, obtain a certification. The crane unit will advise on certified crane operators and the associated fees.

Asbestos-related Work Protocols:

Contractors intending to work with asbestos need to:

- Inform Cal OSHA 24 hours prior, regardless of the asbestos quantity.

- Notify the closest Cal OSHA district office.

- For immediate asbestos work, provide verbal notification, but ensure written confirmation is sent within the next 24 hours.

Regarding asbestos:

- Contractors who disturb over 100 square feet of material containing more than 0.1% asbestos by weight should register yearly with the Asbestos Contractor's Registration Occupational Carcinogen Control Unit.

- Those offering consultation related to such asbestos-rich materials must obtain certification from the Asbestos Consultant and Trainer Approval Unit.

Navigating Business Licensing in California

Every business operating in California, irrespective of its size, location, or type, is obligated to acquire a general business license. This ensures the business operates within the state's legal framework.

Acquiring the License:

For businesses situated in cities, the general business license can be procured from the respective city's licensing office. However, for those based in unincorporated areas or smaller towns governed by the county, the county itself is the licensing authority.

Multiple Locations:

If a business extends its reach across multiple cities within California, it's imperative to have a business license for each city it operates in. This guarantees that the business is legally acknowledged in every city it functions.

Special Provisions for Contractors:

On top of the general license, contractors have an additional licensing layer. They must obtain a specific "contractor's license" which is granted by the Contractor State License Board (CSLB). This license holds validity across California. However, a word of caution: this license doesn't grant permission for contractors to operate beyond California's borders. Contractors wishing to work in other states must adhere to those states' individual licensing protocols.

Understanding the Contractor State License Board (CSLB): Structure, Roles, and Classifications

Introduction to CSLB:

The Contractor State License Board (CSLB) is an essential regulatory body for California's construction industry. Established to bring order and stability, the CSLB now functions under the umbrella of the Department of Consumer Affairs.

CSLB's Organizational Structure:

At the helm of the CSLB is the registrar of contractors, responsible for overseeing the board's administrative policies. This registrar is guided by a 15-member board, comprising 10 public members and five contractors. The governor appoints 11 of these members, with the remaining four appointed by the legislature.

Regular public meetings, hosted by the board throughout the state, allow for open dialogue and contribution from the general public on industry-related matters. Furthermore, the board supervises the functions of its field offices, which include disciplinary actions arising from investigative findings. These investigations often result from complaints lodged against contractors. Additionally, the Statewide Investigative Fraud Team (SWIFT) is dedicated to tracking unlicensed construction activities.

CSLB's Core Functions:

The CSLB's primary mission is to safeguard consumers. This is achieved by fostering policies that prioritize public health, safety, and welfare in the construction sector. The board ensures construction activities uphold the standards of safety, professionalism, and competence. They license contractors and enforce stringent laws, regulations, and standards in a balanced manner.

To support consumers further, the CSLB assists in resolving construction-related disputes and provides valuable information to help consumers make informed choices. Within the realm of contractor's license law, "builder" and "contractor" are terms used to describe those who manage a construction business, engaging in the construction and enhancement of various structures based on their expertise.

Contractor Classifications:

Contractors are grouped into specific classifications based on their trades and skills:

1. **General Engineering Contractor:** Focuses on fixed works requiring specialized engineering expertise.

2. **General Building Contractor:** Primarily oversees the creation and enhancement of structures meant for shelter or enclosure. They manage related trades but have specific bidding restrictions based on the nature of the project and their licenses.

3. **Specialty Contractor:** Specializes in specific trades or crafts, such as electrical or elevator installation. Their work is limited to their licensed classification.

4. **Limited Specialty Contractor:** This encompasses areas outside the standard C2-C60 classifications. Under the C61 category, the CSLB further distinguishes them into D subcategories, like D10 for Elevated Floors and D12 for Synthetic Products.

Licensing and Requirements for Contractors in California

Qualifying Individual

A qualifying individual is a person who is listed on the Contractor's State License Board (CSLB) records as having met the experience and examination requirements for a license. Every license classification issued by the CSLB requires a qualifying individual. A business may hold a single license, but it can encompass multiple classifications, provided that each classification is backed by four years of experience demonstrated by a properly qualified individual, as per state law.

The qualifying individual is accountable for all operations carried out by the licensee and must oversee and control any construction operations performed by the licensee. Any illegal activities conducted by a licensee will impact the qualifying individual and could jeopardize their position. The term "licensee" refers to the business or company that holds a contractor's license.

The types of qualifying individuals permitted for each type of licensee are as follows: for an individual owner or Responsible Managing Employee (RME), for a partnership, a qualifying partner or RME, for a corporation, a Responsible Managing Officer (RMO) or RME, and for a Limited Liability Company (LLC), a Responsible Manager (RM) or Responsible Managing Member (RMM).

If a qualifying individual departs from a company, the business has 90 days to find a replacement. An RME is a full-time employee who works at least 32 hours per week or is present during 80% of the business's operating hours, whichever is less. An RME is also a permanent employee of the licensee with the required work experience. After passing the examination as an RME, the employee may qualify for a license but does not necessarily own a part of the business being licensed.

An RMO is an officer of the business or corporation, such as a president, vice president, secretary, or treasurer. To qualify as an RMO, an individual must demonstrate the required work experience and pass the examination. In both cases, the license is not issued to the qualifying individual, but to the business itself. If the qualifying individual leaves a licensed business, the license remains with the business.

A person may act as a qualifying individual for more than one active license, but only if one of the following conditions exists: there is a common ownership of at least 20% of the equity of each firm for which the person acts as qualifier, the additional firm is a subsidiary of or a joint venture with the first, or the majority of the partners or officers are the same. Even if the individual meets the above conditions, a person may serve as the qualifying individual for no more than three firms in any one year. If a qualified individual separates from a third firm, they must wait one year before associating with a new third firm. In most cases, an RM can act as a qualifying individual for one active license at a time.

Basic Requirements to Become a California Licensed Contractor

All qualifying individuals must be at least 18 years old and capable of effectively managing the daily activities of a construction business. A qualifying individual must also have at least four full years of experience within the last 10 years as a journeyman, foreman, or supervisor in the applied classification. An apprenticeship, college education, or training can account for no more than three years of the required experience.

Who Must Be Licensed?

Any business or individual constructing or altering a building, road, highway, railroad, parking facility, excavation, or any other structures in the state of California that exceeds $500 in labor and materials must be licensed by the California CSLB.

Who is Exempt from Contractor's License?

In some cases, businesses are exempt from the licensing requirement. The following list includes individuals and businesses that are exempt: a project for which the combined value of labor, materials, and all other costs on one or more contracts is less than $500; work on a larger project may not be broken down into smaller amounts less than $500 in an attempt to meet the exemption; an employee who is paid wages, who does not usually work in an independently established business and does not direct or control the work or project; public personnel working on public projects; officers of a court acting within the scope of their office; public utilities working under specified conditions; oil and gas operations performed by an owner or lessee; owner-builders who build or improve existing structures on their own property by performing the work themselves or by using their own employees paid in wages; an owner-builder who owns the property and acts as their own general contractor on the job, either does the work themselves or has employees or subcontractors working on the project. The work site must be their principal place of residence occupied for 12 months prior to completion of the work. The homeowner cannot construct and sell more than two structures within a three-year period; sale or installation of finished products that do not become a fixed part of the structure; a seller of installed carpets holding a retail furniture dealer's license, but then contracts for installation of the carpet with a licensed carpet installer; security alarm company operators licensed by the Bureau of Security and Investigative Services that install, maintain, monitor, sell, alter, or service alarm systems; fire alarm company operators must be licensed by the CSLB; and persons whose activities consist only of installing satellite antenna systems on residential structures or property. These persons must be registered with the Bureau of Electronic and Appliance Repair.

Requirements of Background Checking

All contractor license applicants, officers, partners, owners, and responsible managing employees, as well as home improvement salesperson applicants, are required to submit a full set of fingerprints for a criminal background check. If an applicant has a criminal background related to the construction industry, then CSLB may reject the application. If the CSLB denies the application, the applicant may request a hearing to appeal the decision within 60 days of the date of the denial.

Navigating the Contractor Licensing Process in California

Once a contractor has submitted a comprehensive application that demonstrates adequate work experience, the Contractor State License Board (CSLB) will issue a notice to schedule an examination. The examination process consists of two parts: the law and business segment and a trade-specific examination. However, there is an exception for the limited specialty classification (C-61), which does not require a trade examination.

After successfully passing both segments, the contractor must pay the remaining fees and complete the necessary paperwork to receive their license. If a candidate fails one or both sections or does not appear for the examination, they must reschedule within 90 days and pay an additional rescheduling fee. If this is not done, the application becomes void. The CSLB may grant extensions of up to 90 days if the applicant provides medical documentation explaining their non-appearance or if there are other circumstances beyond the applicant's control.

Applicants have an 18-month period to pass the exam. If they do not pass within this time, the application will be void and they must reapply.

In certain cases, the examination may be waived entirely at the registrar's discretion. This can occur if the applicant has passed both qualifying examinations within the past five years, if the applicant has served as the qualifying individual for another license in good standing in the same classification within the past five years, or if the applicant is an immediate family member of a licensee whose license was active and in good standing for five of the previous seven years following the death or absence of a family member.

The applicant may also be eligible for an examination waiver if they have been engaged in the licensee's business for five of the previous seven years and are applying for the same classification. Additionally, the registrar may waive the examination if they receive written notification that the applicant is licensed as a contractor in another state under a similar classification, provided that state has similar or greater professional qualifications as California.

However, those eligible for an examination waiver must still satisfy the experience requirements of the application. This includes a minimum of five years of journeyman level experience in the business, verified by a qualified person such as an employer, contractor, or other journeymen.

Once a license is obtained, there are several requirements to maintain it. These include posting the necessary bonds, cash deposits, or appropriate license fee. The licensee will receive a pocket license and a wall certificate upon issuance of the license. The pocket license must be carried at all times when acting as a contractor, and the wall certificate must be displayed at the licensee's main place of business at all times. The license number must be included on all advertising.

The license must be renewed before the expiration date to avoid being considered unlicensed. Licenses expire two years from the end of the month in which they were issued. The proper renewal form must be completed and returned to the registrar with the necessary fee before the expiration date.

If a license is not renewed on time and the licensee shows signs of negligence, they may send a written petition to the registrar for a retroactive renewal of the license within 90 days of the expiration date. If the registrar grants the petition, the licensee can avoid operating in an unlicensed period, effectively extending the upcoming regular expiration date.

If renewal does not occur within 90 days of the expiration date, a licensee may renew their license within five years following the most recent expiration date by completing a renewal form and paying the necessary fee, which may include a penalty. If this renewal does not take place within a five-year time period, the license will be considered void. If this occurs, the licensee must file a new application and retake all of the required examinations to receive another license.

A license issued to an individual or specified licensee cannot be transferred or sold. However, certain changes may affect the status of a license. A license may be canceled in the event of the death of an owner, if a general or qualifying partner dies or separates from the business, if there is notification by the licensee of merger, dissolution or surrender of the right to do business in California, or if cancellation, revocation, or withdrawal occurs to any of the businesses forming the joint venture.

In the event of the death of a licensee, their license will be canceled unless a member of their immediate family applies within 90 days of the death for a license continuation. If the registrar grants continuation, the applying family member may continue the previous licensee's contracting business for the period for which the continuance is granted, up to one year. Once this period expires, the family member must obtain their own license to continue business operations.

The same conditions apply if a member of a partnership business dies or leaves the business or if a new partner is added. The license will be canceled, and the remaining partners may request continuation from the registrar within 90 days of the absence of a partner. If the registrar agrees to the continuation, the remaining partners may continue their contracting business during the period for which the continuance is granted, up to one year. To continue the business, the current partners must obtain a new license within 90 days of any change.

A qualifying individual original to the business may qualify for a new license without having to retake the exam. If a licensee loses their qualifying individual, a qualifying individual must be replaced within a 90-day period by another qualifying individual. This individual must pass the examination within the period to keep the license in effect unless the individual meets the waiver requirement.

If a license is surrendered voluntarily at any time by a licensee, the registrar is to order the license canceled and no fee will be returned to the licensee. If a business owned by a licensee has its name or address changed, the registrar must be notified within 90 days.

A licensee that has changed the business style must apply for a new license reflecting this change. Subsequently, two different licenses will be in effect and the licensee may choose to keep both if the qualifying licensee owns a minimum of 20% of both businesses.

A sole proprietorship licensee applying for a corporation license can transfer their existing license number to a corporation. A licensee can request that the license number remain for the corporation if they own a minimum of 51% of the corporation. In this case, the sole proprietorship license will subsequently become void and the corporation will now have the existing license number.

A license can be activated or deactivated by a licensee at any time. When the license is inactive, the licensee is not required to maintain a bond or insurance during this period but must renew the license every four years as opposed to every two years for an active license. To deactivate the license, the licensee must submit to the registrar a form requesting the license to become inactive. If the license is inactive, then the licensee may not perform any contracting operations.

To reactivate the license, another form must be submitted along with a reactivation fee and the necessary bond fees. The fees for reactivation are the same as fees for active renewal.

Guidelines for Contractor Advertising in California

Scope of Contractor Advertising

In California, advertising for licensed contractors isn't limited to just traditional media like newspapers and TV. It spans a vast array of platforms and materials: from business cards, website content, and electronic communications to signage on company vehicles, billboards, brochures, and promotional merchandise with company branding. Even internet postings, directories, or listings suggesting a contractor's availability for work fall under this umbrella.

Mandatory License Number Display

All advertising mediums must prominently display the contractor's license number. Forgetting or omitting this can lead to a civil penalty between $100 and $1000 for first-time offenders.

Vehicle Identification Regulations

For certain specialties, such as C 36 Plumbing, C 45 Sign, and C 57 Well Drilling contractors, specific rules apply. These contractors must display their business name, address, and license number on all sides of their commercial vehicles, with the information written in letters at least 1.5 inches high.

However, all other contractors have a different set of guidelines. They only need to show their business name and contractor license number on their commercial vehicles. This information should be clear and readable, with letters that are a minimum of three-quarters of an inch in both height and width.

Classification-based Advertising Restrictions

It's critical for contractors to only advertise services within their specific licensing classification. For example, a C 29 Masonry contractor advertising electrical services would be committing a violation, unless they also possess a C 10 Electrical contractor license. The lone exceptions to this rule are the licensed A General Engineering and B General Building contractors. They can advertise more broadly as general contractors.

Violating advertising classification guidelines carries a civil penalty between $700 and $1000, on top of any other repercussions determined by the registrar or the court.

The Consequences of Unlicensed Contracting in California

Dangers of Posing as a Legitimate Contractor

Unlicensed contractors, attempting to seem legitimate, often resort to advertising. However, these advertisements, especially if they lack license numbers or display unauthentic numbers not issued by the Contractors State License Board (CSLB), attract CSLB sting operations. Simply put, advertising without a genuine contractor's license number is prohibited.

Specifics for Asbestos Removal Contractors

Contractors who specialize in asbestos removal must adhere to stringent advertising guidelines. Their advertisements must clearly state the contractor's registered license name and feature two crucial numbers: the Asbestos Certification number (provided by CSLB) and the registration number under Labor Code Section 6501.5. Omitting these details can prompt a notice for compliance from the registrar. Further violations, especially advertising without the proper certification, can result in citations and penalties between $100 and $1500.

Penalties for Contracting Without a License

Businesses that engage in contracting without proper licensing face severe repercussions. A first offense might lead to a citation, potential imprisonment of up to six months, and a fine up to $5000. Additional civil penalties ranging from $200 to $15,000 can be imposed, although the registrar might adjust these under specific conditions. More severe actions, like contracting during state-declared emergencies, can lead to criminal charges.

A repeat offense can elevate the situation to criminal levels, with penalties amounting to 20% of the contract price or $5000 (whichever is higher) and potential imprisonment for 90 days. Licensed contractors associating or employing unlicensed individuals, or allowing unlicensed use of their licenses, risk facing up to $15,000 in fines. Deliberately misusing a license number can result in a $10,000 fine and up to a year's imprisonment.

Enforcement Measures by CSLB

To counteract unlicensed activities, the CSLB instituted the Statewide Investigative Fraud Team (SWIFT). This proactive unit can inspect any construction site, even without prior complaints, and ask for proof of licensing. Contractors who fail to produce valid licenses are cited immediately.

If a contractor violates any licensing laws, the registrar can take disciplinary action. Offenses can range from intentional fraud causing substantial harm, deliberate breach of various state laws, to affiliating with previously penalized contractors. Actions against the offender can vary: citations, license revocation or suspension, or even seeking an injunction with the help of legal authorities. An injunction either prohibits certain actions or mandates specific ones, ensuring legal rights are upheld.

Concept Check Questions

1. Which of the following is NOT a responsibility of an effective construction project manager?
   a) Resolving conflicts among project personnel
   b) Monitoring compliance with quality standards
   c) Directly supervising the work crews on site
   d) Maintaining open communication with the owner

2. Which type of management focuses on the technical aspects like budgeting, planning, and monitoring progress?
   a) Executive
   b) Functional
   c) Behavioral
   d) Administrative

3. What is an advantage of using the critical path method for scheduling?
   a) Clearly shows task dependencies
   b) Simple to update manually
   c) Identifies shortest time to completion
   d) Visually displays float time

4. In behavioral management theory, effective delegation involves assigning:
   a) Vague expectations
   b) Limited authority
   c) The entire project workload
   d) Clear responsibility and authority

5. Which term refers to the available time to complete an activity without delaying the overall project?
   a) Free float
   b) Total float
   c) Slack time
   d) Lag time

6. Which business structure offers pass-through taxation to its owners?
   a) Sole proprietorship
   b) Partnership
   c) C Corporation
   d) LLC

7. Which business structure dissolves upon the death or departure of any member?
    a) Sole proprietorship
    b) LLC
    c) Partnership
    d) C Corporation

8. What is required to legally form a C Corporation?
    a) Filing articles of incorporation
    b) Drafting a partnership agreement
    c) Obtaining an EIN from the IRS
    d) Registering a business name

9. What tax disadvantage is associated with a C Corporation?
    a) Self-employment tax on owners
    b) Double taxation on profits and dividends
    c) Pass-through taxation to shareholders
    d) Limitation on deductible business expenses

10. For an excavation 7 feet deep, what permit must a contractor obtain before beginning work?
    a) Tower crane permit
    b) Asbestos work permit
    c) Trenching permit
    d) Scaffolding permit

11. For asbestos-related work, how soon before starting must a contractor notify Cal OSHA?
    a) 48 hours
    b) 24 hours
    c) 12 hours
    d) 1 hour

12. What qualification documentation must a contractor provide to Cal OSHA to secure a construction safety permit?
    a) Proof of insurance
    b) Business license
    c) Injury and Illness Prevention plan
    d) Surety bond

13. What is the minimum depth of an excavation that requires a Cal OSHA trenching permit?
    a) 4 feet
    b) 5 feet
    c) 6 feet
    d) 8 feet

14. If a contractor is working on a project in a California city, which agency issues the required general business license?
    a) California Secretary of State
    b) City licensing department
    c) County licensing office
    d) Contractors State License Board

15. True or False: A contractor licensed in California can automatically work in neighboring states without additional licensing.
    a) True
    b) False

16. Which regulatory body oversees contractor licensing in California?
    a) Contractors Association of California
    b) California Construction Authority
    c) Contractors State License Board
    d) Department of Buildings and Construction

17. Who makes the majority of appointments to the CSLB's 15-member board?
    a) The Governor
    b) The Legislature
    c) The Department of Consumer Affairs
    d) Industry organizations

18. Which contractor classification is limited to work within their specific trade area?
    a) General building contractor
    b) General engineering contractor
    c) Specialty contractor
    d) Limited specialty contractor

19. How many contractor board members are appointed by California's legislature?
    a) 2
    b) 4
    c) 10
    d) 15

20. What is the role of the qualifying individual for a contractor's license?
    a) Oversee daily construction operations
    b) Provide financial backing
    c) Manage human resources
    d) Handle legal compliance

21. What is the maximum number of contractor licenses a qualifying individual can be listed on in a year?
    a) 1
    b) 2
    c) 3
    d) 4

22. If a qualifying individual leaves a licensed business, what happens to the license?
    a) It is terminated
    b) It remains with the business
    c) It transfers to the qualifying individual
    d) It must be reapplied for

23. To qualify as a responsible managing employee, what minimum years of trade experience are required?
    a) 2 years
    b) 3 years
    c) 4 years
    d) 5 years

24. True or False: A qualifying individual can oversee licenses for multiple businesses if there is at least 20% shared ownership.
    a) True
    b) False

25. Where must a contractor's license number be displayed in their advertising?
    a) At the top
    b) In the footer
    c) Prominently
    d) Occasionally

26. What contractors can advertise general contracting services?
    a) C10 Electrical
    b) C46 Solar
    c) A General Engineering
    d) C39 Roofing

27. What is the minimum height for license numbers on most contractor vehicles?
    a) 0.5 inches
    b) 0.75 inches
    c) 1 inch
    d) 1.5 inches

28. Can a licensed plumbing contractor advertise electrical services without holding that license?
    a) Yes
    b) No

29. Which CSLB unit conducts proactive job site inspections for licenses?
    a) Enforcement division
    b) Renewal department
    c) Statewide Investigative Fraud Team
    d) Consumer complaint department

30. Allowing unlicensed use of a contractor's license risks a fine up to:
    a) $5,000
    b) $10,000
    c) $15,000
    d) $20,000

Concept Check Solutions

1. C) Directly supervising the work crews on site. While coordination and communication with workers is important, the project manager does not directly supervise the on-site construction crews. That responsibility falls to the superintendent and foremen. The PM focuses on high-level management.

2. B) Functional. Functional management deals with the technical business aspects like planning, budgeting, scheduling, monitoring progress, and maximizing efficiency. Behavioral management focuses on personnel and human resources.

3. A) Clearly shows task dependencies. A key advantage of the critical path method is it clearly illustrates task dependencies by connecting related activities via flowchart. This reveals the overall sequence of operations.

4. D) Clear responsibility and authority. Effective delegation involves assigning clear responsibility and sufficient authority for tasks. Vague expectations and limited authority hamper delegation.

5. B) Total float. Total float refers to the maximum amount of time an activity can be delayed without affecting the overall project finish date. It is available slack time.

6. B) Partnership. A partnership structure provides pass-through taxation to its partners and owners. This means the business income passes through to the owners' personal tax returns, avoiding double taxation. Sole proprietorships also provide pass-through taxation but are not a separate entity. C Corporations and LLCs do not offer complete pass-through taxation.

7. C) Partnership. Unlike C Corporations and LLCs, partnerships dissolve when any partner departs or passes away. The remaining partners must either liquidate the business or reform a new partnership. Sole proprietorships also dissolve upon the owner's death but do not involve multiple members.

8. A) Filing articles of incorporation. To legally form a C Corporation, articles of incorporation must be filed with the Secretary of State. This establishes the business as a separate legal entity. Partnership agreements, EINs, and business name registrations do not create a C Corporation.

9. B) Double taxation on profits and dividends. C Corporations are subject to double taxation - once at the corporate entity level on profits, and again at the shareholder level on dividends. This is a major disadvantage compared to pass-through taxation structures.

10. C) Trenching permit. For an excavation 7 feet deep, the contractor must obtain a trenching permit from Cal OSHA before beginning the work. Excavations 5 feet or deeper requiring worker entry mandate a trenching permit specifically.

11. B) 24 hours. For asbestos-related work, contractors must notify Cal OSHA 24 hours in advance, regardless of asbestos quantity. This 24 hour notice is mandatory before initiating any asbestos handling or abatement.

12. C) Injury and Illness Prevention plan. To secure any Cal OSHA construction safety permit, the contractor must provide their Injury and Illness Prevention program that details safety protocols. This verifies the contractor's readiness to safely perform the permitted task per regulations.

13. B) 5 feet. The minimum depth of an excavation requiring a Cal OSHA trenching permit is 5 feet. Any trench or excavation 5 feet or deeper into which a worker will enter necessitates this specialized permit beforehand.

14. B) City licensing department. For a contractor working on a project within a California city, the required general business license must be obtained from that specific city's licensing department. City governments issue licenses to operate within their jurisdictions.

15. B) False. A contractor licensed in California cannot automatically work in nearby states. They must follow each state's individual licensing requirements which likely involve getting a separate license for that state. CSLB licensing is valid only in California.

16. C) Contractors State License Board. The Contractors State License Board (CSLB) is the regulatory body that oversees licensing and regulation of contractors in California. They are the sole authority that issues state contractor licenses.

17. A) The Governor. The majority of appointments to the CSLB's 15-member board, 11 members, are made by the Governor of California. Only 4 members are appointed by the state Legislature, so the Governor has the most influence in selecting the CSLB leadership.

18. C) Specialty contractor. Specialty contractors are limited to working within their particular trade or skill area as defined by their license classification. The other contractor types have broader work privileges.

19. B) 4. Out of the 15 CSLB board members, 4 are appointed by California's Legislature while the Governor appoints the other 11. The Legislature has influence but appoints a minority.

20. A) Oversee daily construction operations. The key role of a qualifying individual is overseeing and controlling the daily construction operations and activities conducted under the contractor's license. They are responsible for field supervision.

21. C) 3. The maximum number of contractor licenses a qualifying individual can be listed on in a single year is 3. This limit exists even if the individual meets all the association conditions like shared ownership.

22. B) It remains with the business. If a qualifying individual leaves a licensed contracting business, the license itself remains with the business. It does not transfer or need reapplying for. The business has 90 days to replace the qualifier.

23. C) 4 years. To qualify as a Responsible Managing Employee, an individual must have a minimum of 4 full years of trade experience as a journeyman, foreman, or supervisor within the last 10 years. 2 or 3 years is insufficient.

24. A) True. A qualifying individual can oversee multiple licenses if there is at least 20% shared ownership between the businesses. This is one condition that allows qualifying for multiple entities.

25. C) Prominently. In all advertising materials, a contractor's license number must be prominently displayed. This applies to websites, print ads, billboards, and more. Footers, occasional displays are insufficient.

26. C) A General Engineering. Only contractors who hold an A General Engineering license can advertise full general contracting services. Other classifications must restrict ads to their specialty area.

27. B) 0.75 inches. The minimum height for a contractor's license number on their commercial vehicles is 0.75 inches. Exceptions exist like 1.5 inches for certain specialties.

28. B) No. Unless a plumbing contractor also holds a C10 Electrical license, they cannot legally advertise electrical services. Advertising must match the held classifications.

29. C) Statewide Investigative Fraud Team (SWIFT). SWIFT is the specialized CSLB unit focused on proactively inspecting job sites to check for valid contractor licenses. Renewals, enforcement, and complaints handle licensing reactively after infractions occur.

30. C) $15,000. Licensed contractors who enable unlicensed use of their license risk fines up to $15,000. Maximums of $5000 or $10,000 apply to lesser offenses like incidental lapses.

Business Finances

Navigating Financial Terrain in Contracting

Succeeding in the contracting world hinges not only on superior craftsmanship and effective project management but also on astute financial acumen. This competency doesn't just encompass understanding numbers but also involves a deeper grasp of the financial intricacies intrinsic to the construction industry.

Finance in contracting is akin to the backbone of a structure; it underpins every decision and direction taken. It encompasses the intricate world of accounting, where raw data is transformed into financial statements, balance sheets, and income statements. These meticulously crafted documents shed light on the many facets of a contractor's financial health, from overarching operational costs to the nitty-gritty of individual job costs. Beyond just reflecting past and present monetary statuses, these records are predictive tools. By examining them, contractors can gauge cash flow from past projects and forecast future financial needs.

Starting a contracting business, while exhilarating, is rife with challenges and considerations. This chapter aims to illuminate the financial path, addressing critical aspects that one must contemplate before taking the entrepreneurial plunge:

- **Financial Resources**: This is the bedrock upon which a business stands. Ensuring the availability of resources like machinery, an office, and funds to cover not just operational costs but also personal exigencies is imperative.
- **Risk Factors**: Construction is fraught with uncertainty. From fluctuating material costs and availability to unforeseen regulatory roadblocks and weather disruptions, one must always be prepared for the unexpected.
- **Market Conditions**: Understanding the lay of the land is paramount. Is there enough construction activity in the desired region to justify and sustain a new business?
- **Marketing Strategies**: Building quality structures isn't enough; one must also build a robust clientele base. Formulating effective marketing and networking strategies, especially for public projects, can make all the difference.
- **Specialization**: The world of contracting is vast and varied. From building custom luxurious homes to taking on expansive public works projects, one must pinpoint a niche that aligns with one's strengths and passions.
- **Record Keeping**: This is the unsung hero of contracting. Pristine financial records not only assist in superior planning but can also prove instrumental when wooing potential investors or stakeholders.
- **Reporting Requirements**: Beyond the hands-on tasks, one must be adept at managing and adhering to various reporting protocols, spanning personnel, financial, and legal facets.

In the journey to becoming a successful contractor, the initial steps might seem daunting. But, with a meticulously crafted business plan, fortified by solid financial resources and a clear vision, one can navigate the challenging terrains of the contracting world and erect a business that stands tall and proud.

Tax Obligations and Licensing

Operating a business, especially in the realm of contracting, doesn't just mean managing projects or ensuring profitability. It involves navigating a maze of tax obligations and licensing requirements that vary across federal, state, and local levels. This chapter delves deep into these necessities and aims to provide a clear roadmap for contractors.

1. **Income Taxes - Federal & State**: The US tax system operates on a pay-as-you-go basis. Business owners must estimate the taxes they owe for the year and make payments periodically. The IRS mandates quarterly estimated payments for federal income taxes. Similarly, on the state level, entities like the Franchise Tax Board require estimated state income tax payments. These taxes are based on the income a business anticipates earning in a particular year, and accurate record-keeping is crucial to ensure correct estimations.

2. **Licenses & Permits**: Every construction or renovation project begins with the essential step of acquiring relevant permits. Local authorities, be it city or county, issue these permits, and their costs are intrinsic to business expenses. A failure to secure the necessary permits can lead to legal complications, including fines or even cessation of work. Furthermore, understanding and adhering to zoning laws and building codes is imperative to ensure project success and legality.

3. **Sales and Use Tax**: In states like California, selling tangible goods necessitates acquiring a seller's permit and regularly remitting sales tax. The CDTFA is responsible for managing this process. Contractors, when selling goods, must collect this tax from their customers. In situations where tax on materials was already paid at purchase, it doesn't need to be collected again. The concept of use tax kicks in when goods are sourced from out-of-state, a common occurrence in today's e-commerce era. This tax mirrors the sales tax and is essential to level the playing field between local and out-of-state vendors.

4. **Property Tax**: The realm of property tax isn't just limited to homeowners. Businesses too are liable for property tax. They are taxed on real property, such as land and fixtures, as well as personal property like equipment and supplies. Each year, businesses must submit a Business Property Statement Form (BPS Form), declaring the value of their personal property. Interestingly, while business inventory forms a significant chunk of assets, it's exempt from property tax.

In summary, the contracting world is laden with numerous financial intricacies. Beyond just managing finances, a thorough understanding of tax obligations, licensing protocols, and associated fees is pivotal. Contractors, by staying informed and ensuring compliance, not only safeguard their business operations but also foster trust and reliability among clients.

Cash Management

Cash management is a crucial aspect of any business, including contracting. It involves the careful handling of the company's financial resources, such as the collection of revenue, the concentration of cash, and the investment of liquid assets.

One of the key components of cash management is cash flow. This refers to the tracking of all incoming and outgoing cash transactions, such as payments to suppliers or subcontractors during a construction project. Maintaining a positive cash flow ensures that the contractor has sufficient working capital to complete the job. To achieve this, contractors should keep meticulous records of accounts receivable for all past and ongoing projects.

Accounts receivable is the money owed to the contractor for the goods and services they have provided. To maintain a healthy cash flow, contractors should promptly and regularly send invoices to clients, detailing the payment terms. For example, an invoice might specify "2/10, net 30," suggesting that the client can take a 2% discount if they pay within 10 days, otherwise, the full net amount is due within 30 days.

Notes receivable, on the other hand, is a written promise from a buyer to pay the seller after the sale of products or services. The seller can use these notes to meet current financial obligations. Typically, notes receivable have a longer maturity than accounts receivable, but less than a year. If a buyer fails to pay the owed amount within three months, the seller should send a strongly worded letter with the next invoice, urging immediate payment. If this fails, the contractor may need to engage a collection agency.

Bad debts are another aspect of cash management. These occur when a client fails to pay for credit extended to them. Bad debts can negatively impact cash flow and should be avoided whenever possible. However, the IRS does allow bad debts to be deducted from gross income for tax purposes.

Capitalization is another important concept in cash management. It refers to the funds within a business and how these funds are used for expenses. It also refers to the financial resources available to fund a business, which may include corporate stock, retained earnings, or long-term debt. These financial resources are used to cover necessary business expenses such as tools, vehicles, equipment, office supplies, payroll payments, operating expenses, bonding licenses, and insurance.

At the start of a business, a contractor may obtain funding from two main sources: owner equity and debt financing. Owner equity is the investment of funds by a business owner or stockholder, which includes both paid-in capital and retained earnings. Paid-in capital is the money a business receives from selling shares or part of its ownership, while retained earnings are profits kept for future expenses that are not paid to shareholders as dividends.

Debt financing, on the other hand, involves borrowing funds in the form of bank loans or bond sales. In this case, the business repays the loan with interest after a specified period, without sharing any ownership or control with the lender. This method of financing is often preferred in the early stages of a business, as it does not require giving up any ownership.

Financial Reporting

Financial reporting is the process of disclosing a company's financial information to various stakeholders, including managers, investors, the government, and the general public. This information is typically summarized in the form of a balance sheet and an income statement. These documents record the company's financial gains and losses over a year, providing a comprehensive overview of the company's financial strengths and weaknesses.

The balance sheet, also known as a snapshot, provides a summary of a company's financial position at a specific point in time. It is common for an accountant to provide two balance sheets, detailing the finances of the current year and the previous year. The balance sheet allows stakeholders to understand the company's current and fixed assets, its financial obligations, and the investments made by the owners.

The balance sheet is divided into two sections. The left side lists the company's assets, while the right side details the company's liabilities and the stockholders' equity, also known as the owner's investment. The balance sheet is designed to always balance, meaning the total assets will always equal the total liabilities and stockholders' equity. For example, if a company acquires a piece of equipment worth $15,000, this amount will be added to its assets under property, plant, and equipment, and if financed through a loan, the same amount will be listed as a liability.

Assets include cash, physical goods, and any financial claims the company has on others. Liabilities represent the claims others have on the company. The stockholders' equity section shows the original investment made by the owner and any retained earnings.

Assets are listed in order of declining liquidity, which refers to the speed at which an item can be converted into cash and the company's ability to pay off debt. Current assets, listed at the top left of the balance sheet, include cash or goods that can be easily converted into cash. These may include retentions, accounts receivable, prepaid expenses, and inventories. Fixed assets, such as property and equipment, are listed after current assets.

Here are some definitions of asset terms:

1. **Cash**: This refers to liquid funds or money the company has on hand or in the bank.
2. **Retentions**: These are specified amounts, typically 10%, withheld from progress payments to the contractor until the project is finally accepted.
3. **Accounts Receivable**: This is money owed to the company by customers for completed construction projects.
4. **Inventory**: This includes labor, materials used, and both direct and indirect overhead on jobs that are still in progress.
5. **Prepaid Expenses**: These are future expenses paid in advance for later value, such as insurance premiums. They are recorded as assets on the balance sheet until the expenses expire or are incurred.
6. **Fixed Assets**: These are physical resources owned or obtained by the contractor for use in their job operations, which will not be resold. They are valued at the original cost less accumulated depreciation.
7. **Other Assets**: These include any resources not listed in the previous categories, such as scrap materials, equipment held for resale, long-term receivables, and intangible assets like trademarked logos or goodwill.
8. **Accumulated Depreciation**: This is the cumulative sum of all depreciation expenses previously recorded for assets. It is also known as a contra account, which is an account linked to another

account with an opposite normal balance and is reported as a balance subtraction of the other account.

Understanding Depreciation

Depreciation is an accounting method that assigns a cost to a fixed asset over its lifespan. There are two primary methods of calculating depreciation: straight-line depreciation and accelerated depreciation.

Straight-line depreciation assumes that a fixed asset loses an equal amount of value after each accounting period, typically a year. The annual depreciation is calculated by subtracting the residual value of a fixed asset from the original asset cost, then dividing that value by its useful life. The formula for calculating straight-line depreciation is: Depreciation per year = (Original cost - Residual value) / Useful life of fixed asset. The residual value, also known as salvage value, is the estimated amount that can be gained from the resale of a fixed asset after its useful life.

For example, if a company invests in office equipment worth $20,000 with an estimated useful life of ten years and a residual value of $2,000, the depreciation per year using the straight-line method would be ($20,000 - $2,000) / 10, which equals $1,800. The asset will decrease in value by $1,800 each year. If the asset is only used for three months of the year, the depreciation for that year would be a quarter of $1,800, or $450.

Accelerated depreciation, on the other hand, allows for faster deductions in the early years of a fixed asset's useful life. This method is often used to reduce tax liabilities in the early life of a fixed asset.

Liabilities are obligations to pay money or other assets, or to render future services. They are divided into two categories on the balance sheet: current liabilities and long-term liabilities. Current liabilities include company debts that must be paid within a year of the balance sheet date, while long-term liabilities are notes or mortgages due more than one year in the future.

Understanding the relationship between current and fixed assets and current and long-term liabilities is crucial for analyzing financial statements. Current liabilities can include accounts payable, notes payable, accrued expenses payable, accrued payroll, miscellaneous taxes payable, and federal income tax payable.

Stockholders' equity, also known as net worth, represents the owner's claim on the business assets resulting from the owner's investment. Capital stock is the total amount invested in the business by a contractor and/or investors in exchange for a share of common stock at the par value. Retained earnings are the total corporate earnings minus the total declared dividends since the establishment of the corporation.

Cash vs. Accrual Accounting: Choosing the Right Method for Your Construction Business

When it comes to accounting, businesses, especially in construction, often choose between two primary methods: cash and accrual. Let's break down these methods to help you understand them better:

1. **Cash Method of Accounting:**

   - In this approach, revenues are recorded when you receive payments and expenses are recorded when you make payments.

   - This method is popular among small businesses because of its simplicity.

   - However, be cautious: this method can sometimes distort the actual financial picture of a business. As a result, the IRS frequently reviews businesses using this method.

2. **Accrual Method of Accounting:**

   - Here, revenues and expenses are recorded when transactions occur, regardless of when the money changes hands.

   - This is often the recommended method for many construction businesses.

   - For example, if you incur an expense for construction materials on October 20th, 2020, but pay the supplier on November 5th, 2020:

     - Under the cash method, this would be recorded as a November expense (because that's when the cash was paid).

     - Under the accrual method, it would be an October expense (because the materials were received in October).

3. **Special Considerations for Long-Term Projects:**

   - **Completed Contract Method:** This method records the entire profit or loss from a project only when it's finished. This might sound good because you can delay tax payments. However, the downside is that this method can sometimes make financial records unclear. Plus, you can only account for losses after the project ends.

   - **Percentage of Completion Method:** This method involves updating your books based on the progress of a project. For instance, if you've completed 25% of a project and incurred 25% of the estimated costs, then you'd record 25% of the expected revenue for that project. The catch? This method heavily relies on estimates, which can vary from the actual results. To calculate the completion percentage, use this formula: Percentage of completion = (Costs incurred so far) / (Total estimated project costs).

Knowing the difference between these accounting methods is crucial for construction business owners. Choosing the right method can significantly impact your financial reports and tax obligations.

Essential Financial Ratios for Construction Companies

This chapter delves into key financial metrics essential for construction companies, ensuring they remain solvent and competitive. These metrics also play a crucial role in the CSLB contractors license exam.

1. **Current Ratio:** This ratio provides a snapshot of a company's short-term liquidity by comparing its current assets to its current liabilities.

    - **Formula:** Current Ratio = Current Assets / Current Liabilities.

    - **Example:** If a company has $200,000 in current assets and faces $100,000 in current liabilities, the current ratio is 2.0. This indicates that the company has $2 in assets for every dollar it owes within the next year. A ratio above one is favorable as it shows the company's assets surpass its liabilities.

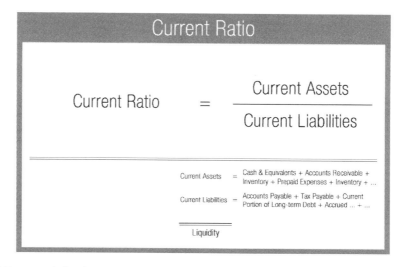

2. **Quick Ratio (Acid Test Ratio):** This ratio evaluates a company's immediate ability to cover its liabilities without relying on the sale of inventory.

    - **Formula:** Quick Ratio = (Current Assets - Inventory) / Current Liabilities.

    - **Interpretation:** A 0.75 quick ratio indicates that for every dollar of debt, the company has 75 cents in assets that can be quickly converted to cash. A value of 1.0 or above is typically seen as healthy, but standards can vary by industry. Companies with low quick ratios may find it difficult to secure credit or loans.

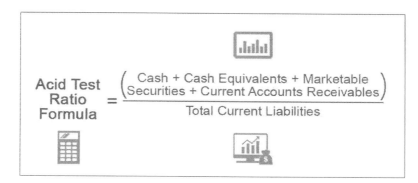

3. **Working Capital:** This measurement reveals the net amount of a company's liquid assets.

- **Formula:** Working Capital = Current Assets - Current Liabilities.

- **Example:** If a company's current assets amount to $300,000, and it faces $150,000 in liabilities, it has a positive working capital of $150,000. Positive working capital signifies that a company has excess assets to reinvest and expand. On the other hand, negative working capital suggests possible over-leverage and a shortage of funds for growth. Inadequate working capital is a frequent stumbling block for many small businesses, underscoring the importance of prudent financial management.

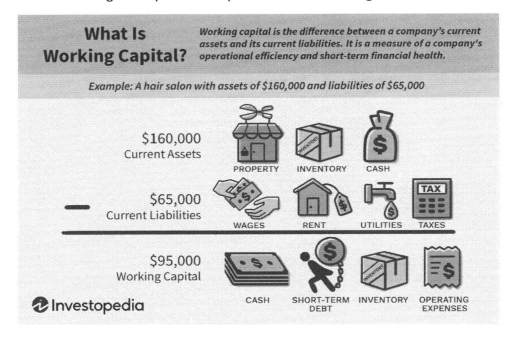

Decoding the Income Statement: An Overview for Contractors

An income statement, often termed as the profit and loss (P&L) statement, offers a glimpse into a company's financial health during a specified time frame, like a year, quarter, or month. Essentially, it provides a breakdown of what a business earned and what it spent.

1. **Revenues:** The top line of the income statement shows the business's total earnings, often labeled as sales, net sales, or sale revenue. This is the total amount billed to customers for various projects.

2. **Operating Costs:** This section breaks down the expenses involved in conducting business. They include:

    - **Direct Labor:** This covers the wages paid for all tasks carried out during the given period. It's essential for gauging company profitability and worker productivity.

    - **Direct Labor Burden:** This encompasses all additional expenses linked to the labor payroll, including items like payroll taxes, insurance, and employee benefits. If employees are part of a union, associated costs, such as union dues, are also included here.

    - **Materials:** Often the heftiest expense on the statement, materials pertain to all the resources used in projects. Given its sizeable impact on costs, it's vital to manage and oversee this account meticulously.

    - **Other Direct Costs:** These are project-specific expenses not listed earlier, including permits, insurance, equipment rentals, and bond costs.

    - **Administrative and General Expenses:** These costs aren't tied to specific jobs but are necessary for overall business operations.

3. **Pretax Income:** After subtracting all the operating expenses from revenue, we get the 'income before federal income tax' or pretax income. For corporations, this is the amount upon which federal taxes are calculated. Sole proprietorships and partnerships, however, report this income on the individual tax returns of the owners.

4. **Net Income (Net Profit):** This is the final number on the income statement, showcasing the company's profitability after all expenses. It's the difference between revenues and total expenses, including taxes, if they apply. Often termed the "bottom line," it's a crucial indicator of a company's financial health.

Concept Check Questions

1. What key metric on a balance sheet provides insight into a contractor's debt obligations?
   a) Accounts receivable
   b) Accounts payable
   c) Retained earnings
   d) Gross profit margin

2. What reporting requirements relate to employee payroll taxes and workers compensation?
   a) OSHA
   b) Filing taxes
   c) Permit applications
   d) Material orders

3. What strategy is key for building clientele as a new contractor?
   a) Website development
   b) Marketing tactics
   c) Hiring superintendents
   d) Ordering materials

4. Who is responsible for collecting and remitting sales tax on goods sold in California?
   a) Seller
   b) Buyer
   c) California BOE
   d) City officials

5. What form must businesses submit annually to declare taxable personal property holdings?
   a) Schedule C
   b) 1099-MISC
   c) Business Property Statement
   d) Franchise Tax Return

6. Which business asset is exempt from state property taxes?
   a) Real estate
   b) Equipment
   c) Supplies
   d) Inventory

7. What is indicated when an invoice states "net 30" terms?
   a) 30% discount if paid early
   b) 30% deposit required
   c) Payment due in 30 days
   d) 30 days late fee applies

8. What is a written promise by a client to pay the contractor after delivery of services?
   a) Accounts payable
   b) Capitalization
   c) Note receivable
   d) Security deposit

9. What financing option involves borrowing funds and repaying with interest but no loss of ownership?
   a) Debt financing
   b) Venture capital
   c) Crowdfunding
   d) Angel investing

10. What IRS tax deduction helps offset the negative effects of bad debts?
    a) Rent expenses
    b) Cost of goods sold
    c) Bad debt deduction
    d) Depletion

11. What is the term for financial resources available to fund business operations and assets?
    a) Revenue
    b) Equity
    c) Capitalization
    d) Profits

12. What balance sheet section shows the original investments made by the business owners?
    a) Liabilities
    b) Assets
    c) Stockholders' equity
    d) Working capital

13. Which item is classified as a current asset on a contractor's balance sheet?
    a) Company vehicle
    b) Retainage receivable
    c) Office building
    d) Construction equipment

14. A contractor's unpaid supplier invoices would appear in which balance sheet category?
    a) Accounts receivable
    b) Other current assets
    c) Accounts payable
    d) Notes payable

15. Which balance sheet factor considers both assets and liabilities?
    a) Liquidity
    b) Working capital
    c) Equity
    d) Income

16. What depreciation method calculates an equal deduction over each period of an asset's useful life?
    a) Straight-line
    b) Accelerated
    c) Declining balance
    d) Double-declining

17. If a contractor uses an asset for half of the accounting year, how much depreciation should be recorded?
    a) The full annual amount
    b) Half of the annual amount
    c) A quarter of the annual amount
    d) None for that year

18. What balance sheet component represents the owner's claim on business assets?
    a) Working capital
    b) Accounts receivable
    c) Stockholders' equity
    d) Inventory

19. What method records expenses when payments are made by the contractor?
    a) Cash method
    b) Accrual method
    c) GAAP principles
    d) Markup accounting

20. Under the accrual method, when is revenue recorded for a project invoice sent in December but paid in January?
    a) December
    b) January
    c) The following year
    d) When the check is received

21. What is a disadvantage of using the completed contract method for long-term projects?
    a) Tax payments are delayed
    b) Revenue is recorded incrementally
    c) Losses can only be recorded at completion
    d) Estimates are required

22. What calculation is used to determine the completion percentage for the percentage of completion method?
    a) Costs to date ÷ Total revenue
    b) Payments to date ÷ Total costs
    c) Costs to date ÷ Total estimated costs
    d) Revenue to date ÷ Total revenue

23. Which accounting method can sometimes distort the true financial status of a business?
    a) Accrual method
    b) Cash method
    c) LIFO method
    d) Percentage of completion

24. What ratio calculates a company's ability to pay short-term debts from current assets?
    a) Debt ratio
    b) Current ratio
    c) Quick ratio
    d) Return on assets

25. A high current ratio indicates a company has:
    a) Excess inventory
    b) Financial issues
    c) Ample liquidity
    d) High liabilities

26. A quick ratio of 0.8 means a company has _____ in liquid assets per $1 of liability.
    a) $0.80
    b) $1.25
    c) $2.00
    d) $5.00

27. If current assets are $500,000 and current liabilities are $300,000, working capital is:
    a) $100,000
    b) $200,000
    c) $300,000
    d) $500,000

28. Negative working capital indicates:
    a) Excess inventory
    b) Ample liquidity
    c) Potential overleverage
    d) High profitability

29. Which financial metric specifically excludes inventory from its calculation?
    a) Debt ratio
    b) Current ratio
    c) Working capital
    d) Quick ratio

30. On an income statement, where are the wages paid to workers for project tasks shown?
    a) Cost of goods sold
    b) Operating expenses
    c) Direct labor
    d) Administrative costs

31. Permit fees for a specific construction project are considered what type of expense?
    a) Direct labor
    b) Materials
    c) Other direct costs
    d) Administrative

32. What income statement section shows company earnings before accounting for taxes?
    a) Gross profit
    b) Net profit
    c) Pretax income
    d) Operating income

33. General company costs like office supplies and utilities are categorized under what expense?
    a) Direct materials
    b) Direct labor
    c) Administrative
    d) Equipment

34. What key metric indicates the overall profitability of a company after expenses?
    a) Gross income
    b) Net income
    c) Revenue
    d) Retained earnings

35. If a contractor has $200,000 in revenues and $150,000 in total expenses, their net income is:
    a) $50,000
    b) $150,000
    c) $200,000
    d) $350,000

Concept Check Solutions

1. B) Accounts payable. A company's accounts payable balance on their balance sheet provides insight into current debt obligations for purchased goods/services. Receivables, retained earnings, and margins reflect other financial aspects.

2. B) Filing taxes. Contractors must comply with reporting requirements related to employee payroll taxes, workers comp insurance etc. when filing business taxes. OSHA, permits, orders are unrelated.

3. B) Marketing tactics. Implementing effective marketing tactics to build a strong clientele base is imperative when starting as a new contractor trying to establish a reputation.

4. A) Seller. In California, the seller of tangible goods is responsible for collecting and remitting the associated sales tax. This includes contractors selling goods. The buyer pays it, but the seller remits it based on transactions.

5. C) Business Property Statement. Businesses must annually submit a Business Property Statement declaring their taxable personal property holdings like equipment and machinery. Other forms relate to income taxes and employee reporting.

6. D) Inventory. Of key business assets, inventory is exempt from state property tax in California. Real estate, equipment, and supplies are subject to property tax and must be reported.

7. C) Payment due in 30 days. The "net 30" terms on an invoice indicate the client must pay the net amount owed within 30 days from the invoice date. It does not refer to discounts, deposits, or late fees.

8. C) Note receivable. A note receivable is a written promise by a client to pay the contractor after delivery of services rendered. Other choices do not depict this scenario.

9. A) Debt financing. With debt financing, funds are borrowed and repaid with interest, without the loss of any business ownership or control that equity financing would incur.

10. C) Bad debt deduction. The IRS allows businesses to deduct qualified bad debts from gross income to help offset negative impacts. Other choices like rent or depletion are unrelated.

11. C) Capitalization. Capitalization refers specifically to the financial resources available to fund business assets, operations, and expenses. Revenue, equity, and profits have different meanings.

12. C) Stockholders' equity. The stockholders' equity section of the balance sheet shows the original capital investments made by the owners of the business. Assets are owned resources, liabilities are owed, and working capital is assets minus liabilities.

13. B) Retainage receivable. Retainage receivable is considered a current asset on a contractor's balance sheet because retainage is typically received within one year after project completion. Vehicles, buildings, and equipment are fixed assets.

14. C) Accounts payable. Unpaid supplier invoices owed by a contractor would appear under accounts payable on the balance sheet, as this liability account tracks money owed to vendors.

15. B) Working capital. Working capital considers both current assets and current liabilities, making it a balance sheet factor that incorporates assets and liabilities. Other choices do not include both.

16. A) Straight-line. Straight-line depreciation calculates an equal deduction amount over each period of an asset's useful life. Accelerated depreciation allows for faster deductions early on.

17. B) Half of the annual amount. If a contractor uses an asset for half of the accounting year, the depreciation recorded should be half of the full annual depreciation amount. Recording the full amount or a quarter amount would be incorrect.

18. C) Stockholders' equity. Stockholders' equity represents the owner's financial claim on the business assets resulting from their investments. It is not an asset itself like accounts receivable or inventory.

19. A) Cash method. Under the cash method of accounting, expenses are recorded when actual payments are made by the contractor to vendors or suppliers. The accrual method records expenses when they are incurred, not necessarily when paid. GAAP principles are accounting standards, not methods. Markup accounting involves pricing formulas.

20. A) December. Under the accrual accounting method, revenue is recorded when the transaction occurs, not when payment is received. So for a project invoice sent in December that is paid in January, the revenue is recorded in December when invoiced. Cash method would record it in January upon payment.

21. C) Losses can only be recorded at completion. A disadvantage of the completed contract method is that any losses on a long-term project can only be accounted for when the entire project is finished. Revenue is not recorded incrementally, payments are delayed, and estimates are not required under this method.

22. C) Costs to date ÷ Total estimated costs. The percentage of completion is calculated by taking the costs incurred to date divided by the total estimated costs for the full project duration. Revenue, payments, and total revenue do not factor into this formula.

23. B) Cash method. The cash method of accounting can sometimes distort the true financial status of a business because it records revenues and expenses based on cash transactions, not necessarily when transactions and work occur. The accrual method more accurately matches revenues with expenses.

24. B) Current ratio. The current ratio calculates a company's ability to pay short-term debts from current assets by comparing current assets to current liabilities. It shows short-term liquidity. Debt ratio, quick ratio, and ROA do not specifically measure short-term solvency.

25. C) Ample liquidity. A high current ratio indicates a company has ample liquidity and healthy short-term solvency, with sufficient current assets to cover debts due within a year. It does not necessarily mean excess inventory, financial issues, or high overall liabilities.

26. A) $0.80. A quick ratio of 0.8 means the company has $0.80 in readily convertible assets per $1 of current liability. It does not mean $1.25, $2, or $5 per $1 as the ratio is less than 1.

27. B) $200,000. With $500,000 in current assets and $300,000 in current liabilities, working capital is $500,000 - $300,000 = $200,000. Subtracting current liabilities from current assets yields working capital.

28. C) Potential overleverage. Negative working capital indicates potential overleverage, lack of liquidity, and insufficient funds to reinvest into growth. It does not indicate excess inventory, ample liquidity, or high profitability.

29. D) Quick ratio. The quick ratio specifically excludes inventory from current assets when measuring a company's solvency, since inventory cannot immediately pay debts. Other ratios include all current assets.

30. C) Direct labor. On a contractor's income statement, the wages paid to workers for tasks carried out on projects are categorized under direct labor. Cost of goods sold is irrelevant, operating expenses are too broad, and administrative costs are overhead.

31. C) Other direct costs. Permit fees required for a specific construction project are considered other direct costs on the income statement, as they tie directly to that project but are not labor or materials.

32. C) Pretax income. Pretax income on an income statement shows a company's earnings before accounting for taxes. Net profit and operating income are after-tax figures. Gross profit is revenue minus cost of goods sold.

33. C) Administrative. General company costs like office supplies and utilities are administrative expenses on an income statement, as they are not tied to specific projects but required for overall operations.

34. B) Net income. Net income, also called net profit, indicates a company's overall profitability after subtracting all operating expenses from revenues. It shows the final bottom line earnings.

35. A) $50,000. With $200,000 in revenues and $150,000 in total expenses, the net income is $200,000 - $150,000 = $50,000. Net income is revenues minus total expenses.

Employment Requirements
Navigating Employee Rights and Hiring Laws in California

This chapter delves into the intricacies of the hiring process in California, emphasizing the legal landscape governing employer-employee relationships. A grasp of these laws is fundamental for contractors and budding businesses in the state.

1. **California Labor Code:** Central to employee rights in California, this code, accessible via the California Labor and Workforce Development Agency website, encapsulates employment regulations. It serves as a shield against possible employer misdemeanors. The Division of Labor Standards Enforcement, under the Department of Industrial Relations, oversees its enforcement and can inspect any Californian employment establishment.

2. **Unfair Employment Practices:** The code condemns practices like:

    - Discrimination based on group membership during hiring, firing, training, or pay.

    - Coercing or threatening employees over their political choices.

    - Making union non-participation a job requirement.

    - Punishing employees for participating in discrimination proceedings.

3. **Protection from Discrimination and Harassment:** The Department of Fair Employment and Housing (DFEH) and the California Fair Employment and Housing Act champion the rights of workers against illegal discrimination and harassment. It's the employer's responsibility to ensure a workplace free from such issues, encompassing factors from race and gender to age and military status.

4. **Hiring Guidelines:** Finding the right fit for a job isn't just about skills; it's about integrity and commitment. While the right candidate boosts productivity and morale, a misfit can jeopardize business success. Moreover:

    - Every employee's employment eligibility should be verified per the Immigration and Nationality Act.

    - The I-9 forms, required by the Immigration and Naturalization Service, should be maintained for at least three years post-hire or a year post-employment termination.

5. **Americans With Disabilities Act (ADA):** Employers with a team of 15 or more should be ADA-compliant. The act champions the rights of those with significant physical or mental impediments, prohibiting discrimination across all job facets.

6. **Whistleblower Protection:** California shields its workers, both in public and private sectors, from backlash after they spotlight potential legal breaches by their employers.

7. **Onboarding Requirements:** During the hiring process, it's imperative to:

    - Obtain the employee's social security number.

    - Ensure the employee completes the federal W-4 form.

    - Authenticate their identity and work authorization in the U.S. using the I-9 form.

Staying abreast of these guidelines and regulations is pivotal for businesses to foster trust, ensure compliance, and promote a harmonious work environment.

Understanding California Labor Code: Workweek Norms and Child Labor Protections

The California State Labor Code provides detailed guidelines about workweek standards, overtime, breaks, and child labor provisions. Here's a concise breakdown:

Workweek & Overtime:

- **Standard Workweek:**

  - Typically five days, with each day being eight hours.

  - Cannot exceed 40 hours in total, though variations are allowed based on employee agreements.

- **Overtime Provisions:**

  - Overtime is mandatory for hours exceeding the standard eight-hour day or 40-hour workweek.

  - Basic overtime rate: 1.5 times the standard pay rate.

  - 12+ hours in a day: Double the standard pay rate.

  - If working seven consecutive days:

    - First eight hours on the seventh day require 1.5 times regular pay.

    - More than eight hours on the seventh day requires double pay.

  - Exceptions: Employees working less than 30 hours in a week or six hours on a day.

Rest & Break Periods:

- **Rest Breaks:**

  - Every four hours warrants a 10-minute paid break.

  - Separate rest facilities required, distinct from restrooms.

  - If the daily work time is under three and a half hours, breaks aren't necessary.

- **Lunch Breaks:**

  - 5+ hour workdays require a 30-minute lunch break (waivable for <6 hours).

  - This break is unpaid unless an agreement is in place.

  - 10+ hour workdays necessitate a second 30-minute break (waivable under certain conditions).

Employing Minors:

- **Permits & Restrictions:**

  - Most under 18 need a work permit, and employers must possess a valid employment permit.

- Work permits often come from the minor's school and expire shortly after a new school year begins.

- Work hours are restricted based on age:

  - **Ages 14-15:**

    - Can work three hours on school days or eight hours on non-school days, capped at 18 hours weekly.

    - Allowed roles: Office, clerical, or sales.

    - Hazardous work restrictions in place.

  - **Ages 16-17:**

    - Four hours permissible on school days or eight hours on non-school days, maxing at 48 hours weekly.

- **Wages & Compliance:**

  - Minors are entitled to the minimum wage and overtime rates set by the California Industrial Welfare Commission.

  - Employers must maintain permits, subject to inspections by authorized personnel.

  - Non-compliance fines: Up to $500 for initial offenses.

Wage Regulations

According to the California Labor Code, employers are required to display a notice in the workplace that details the place and time of wage payments. Employers must pay their employees at least twice a month. Furthermore, employers are responsible for the costs of any necessary pre-employment medical examinations, and these costs should not be deducted from the employees' wages.

It is prohibited for an employer and employee to agree on any arrangement where a portion of the employee's wages are returned to the employer as a kickback. However, employers are allowed to deduct costs related to life insurance, medical plans, retirement plans, or similar programs from an employee's wages, provided they have the employee's written consent.

Employees have the right to terminate their employment at any time. If an employee quits without notice, their wages are due and payable within 72 hours. If an employee gives 72 hours notice before quitting, or if an employer lays off an employee, their wages are due immediately.

Employees are allowed to file a complaint with the labor commissioner if their employer fails to pay any due wages. Employers cannot take disciplinary action against an employee for filing such a complaint. If an employer willfully fails to pay legally due wages, they may be liable for all wages and up to 30 days additional wages as a penalty. They may also face a fine of $50 for a first violation or a fine of $100 plus 25% of the unpaid wages for any subsequent violations.

If an employer issues a wage check that bounces due to insufficient funds or a nonexistent account, they will be liable to a penalty of a maximum of 30 days additional wages. This penalty period can end prior to the 30-day deadline if the employer pays the employee or if the employee files a lawsuit to recover lost wages. This penalty can be waived if the employer can prove the error was unintentional.

Regarding paid sick leave, an employee accrues one hour for every 30 hours worked, starting from their first day of employment. However, they can only start using it after the 90th day of employment. Generally, the law requires employers to provide and allow employees to use at least 24 hours or three days of paid sick leave per year. Employers can choose to implement a paid sick leave policy as accrual or no accrual upfront payment laws.

Certain labor laws not included in the California Labor Code apply primarily to positions financed or assisted by the federal government. The Davis-Bacon Act mandates that employers pay employees a prevailing wage on federal projects. The Walsh-Healy Public Contracts Act specifies minimum wages, overtime, and safety and health standards on contracts exceeding $10,000 that provide materials, supplies, articles, or equipment to the federal government. The Contract Work Hours and Safety Standards Act sets overtime and safety standards for contractors and subcontractors with federal service contracts and federally funded and assisted construction contracts over $100,000.

All employers are responsible for withholding and paying both federal income tax and Social Security (FICA) taxes if they have one or more employees. Employers must obtain an Employer Identification Number (EIN) for identification purposes on federal tax returns. Federal income tax and FICA must be withheld from the employees' wages and paid on a quarterly, monthly, or semi-monthly basis as required.

Employers are responsible for withholding and/or matching the following federal payroll taxes: federal income tax, which is withheld from all employees unless exempt, and Social Security and Medicare taxes (FICA), which are based on a percentage of an employee's wages with a matching employer contribution.

Employers must submit quarterly federal employment tax returns to the IRS, calculating the total federal income taxes and Social Security taxes withheld from the employee wages during that specific period, along with the amount of Social Security tax to be paid by the employer. If the amount withheld exceeds the mandated limit, the employer may have to make more frequent deposits than the regular quarterly tax returns rate.

Employers must also pay a Federal Unemployment Tax (FUTA) if they employed one or more employees in 20 or more different calendar weeks in a given year, or if wages of $1,500 or more were paid in any calendar quarter of a given year. The FUTA tax must be paid by the employer and cannot be withheld from the employee's wages. An annual FUTA return must be filed separately from the returns filed for federal income tax and FICA. The employer is responsible for a percentage of the first $7,000 paid to the employee for the calendar year.

Employment Tax Obligations in California: A Comprehensive Guide for Employers

In California, employers are required to adhere to specific guidelines related to employment taxes, state payroll, and unemployment insurance tax. Here's a breakdown of these obligations:

Registration with the EDD:

- Employers should register with the Employment Development Department (EDD) within 15 days of paying over $100 in taxable wages.

- Upon registration, an identification number is provided for use on state tax returns and other communications.

Electronic Submission Requirements (Assembly Bill 1245):

- Employers must electronically submit employment tax returns, wage reports, and payroll tax deposits to the EDD.

Breakdown of State Payroll Taxes:

1. **State Personal Income Tax (PI):**

   - Withheld from employee wages.

   - Based on the W-4 or D-4 withholding allowance certificate form.

2. **State Disability Insurance (SDI):**

   - Deducted from employee wages, based on a percentage of gross earnings.

   - SDI provides compensation for employees incapacitated due to injury or illness.

   - Self-employed individuals can voluntarily enroll by paying premiums based on IRS quarterly reporting.

3. **State Unemployment Insurance (U):**

   - Employers may need to pay this tax, with the rate determined by the unemployment claims of former employees.

4. **State Employment Training Tax (ETT):**

   - Intended to boost business and the state's economy.

   - Employers contribute 1/10 of 1% on the first $7000 paid to each employee annually.

Filing Requirements:

- Quarterly employment state tax returns must be filed with the EDD by the end of the month following a quarter. For instance, Q1 returns are due by April 30th.

- Employers must issue W-2 forms for employees with income, Social Security, or Medicare tax deductions by January 31st of the following year.

- Contractors should provide 1099 forms documenting untaxed earnings:

- 1099-MISC forms for subcontractors who received over $600 should be sent by January 31st.
- The form must be submitted to the IRS by February 28th (mail) or March 31st (e-filing).

Penalties:

- Late or incorrect filing of W-2 or 1099-MISC forms results in penalties:
    - $50 for each form filed within 30 days.
    - $100 if filed by August 1st.
    - $260 if filed post-August 1st or if forms contain errors.

Net Pay & Record Keeping:

- **Net Pay:** Represents an employee's earnings after deductions. It's calculated as: Net pay = Gross pay - Taxes and deductions. Employers should provide a statement with each paycheck detailing this calculation.
- **Records Retention:** Employers must retain employment and tax records for at least four years. This includes:
    - Basic employee details, federal EIN, state identification number, and sales/use tax account number.
    - Dates, amounts of all wage payments, and tax deposits made.
    - Employee tax withholding certificates (W-4 form) and records related to sickness or injury payments.
- Payroll records should be kept for three years post-termination, while records like time cards, wage rate tables, and wage additions or deductions need to be retained for two years.

Employment Termination and Rights in California

Termination of employment in California can arise from either an employee's decision to resign or an employer's decision to dismiss an employee.

Employee Resignation: When an employee chooses to resign, they can legally do so at any time. The timing of their final wage payment is determined by the notice given:

- If no advance notice is provided, the employer must pay the employee's wages within 72 hours of departure.

- If at least 72 hours notice is given, wages are payable at the time of resignation.

Employer Dismissal: Employers have a legal right, as outlined in the California State Labor Code, to expect satisfactory job performance. If an employee underperforms or engages in misconduct, the employer can terminate their employment. In such scenarios, due wages must be promptly paid at the time of termination.

California Employment Notices Poster: Workplaces must prominently display the California Employment Notices Poster, ensuring visibility for all employees. This poster covers various employment laws, including those related to voting time off, military leave, and the Family Medical Leave Act (FMLA).

Voting Rights: Per the California Elections Code, employers must display a notice at least 10 days before an election, allowing employees up to two hours of paid leave to vote. This provision applies when employees lack adequate time outside working hours. Employees should notify employers two days before the election if they plan to use this provision.

Rights for Service Members and Their Families: The Uniformed Services Employment and Reemployment Rights Act (USERRA) and the Military Family Leave Act safeguard service members and their families' rights. Key features include:

- Reemployment rights after returning from uniformed services.

- 12 weeks of leave for emergencies involving a close family member on active duty.

- 26 weeks of leave to care for a relative injured in service.

- Prohibiting discrimination based on military service.

Family Medical Leave Act (FMLA): FMLA ensures eligible employees of qualifying employers can avail up to 12 weeks of unpaid, job-protected leave annually while retaining group health insurance. Reasons can include childbirth, child adoption or fostering, caring for a family member with serious health issues, or the employee's health condition, including pregnancy. Employers are covered by FMLA if they employ 50 or more people during at least 20 weeks in the current or preceding year.

Understanding Labor Unions and Employee Rights: Key Provisions and Regulations

Labor unions play a pivotal role in the labor code, championing employees' rights to either associate with an existing union or establish a new one. Here's a breakdown of the fundamental aspects of labor unions and related rights:

1. Union Membership and Employer Conduct:

- Employers cannot obstruct employees from affiliating with a union or discriminate against members or organizers.

- The Fair Employment and Housing Act mandates that job applicants cannot be compelled to join a union as a precondition for employment. However, post-hiring, employers may stipulate union membership.

2. Collective Bargaining Agreements (CBAs):

- A CBA is a negotiated contract between a union and an employer.

- If breached, the erring party is susceptible to legal repercussions.

- If the business undergoes a sale or transfer, the CBA typically becomes void unless it carries a 'successor clause'. This clause would bind the new owner to the agreement, effective for three years from the CBA's start date or its expiration date, whichever is earlier.

3. Resolving Labor Disputes:

- Should union representatives and employers fail to agree on a contract, a labor dispute may arise. Responses include:

    - **Strike:** Employees withhold labor until a satisfactory agreement is finalized.

    - **Lockout:** Employers prevent employees from accessing the workplace until a resolution is achieved.

- The National Labor Relations Act (NLRA) safeguards non-federal and non-state workers during strikes intended to ameliorate work conditions. Under the NLRA:

    - Employers can't menace employees with job termination, benefits cuts, or the threat of closing down during a strike or lockout.

    - Employers are, however, permitted to recruit interim replacements during a strike but must adhere to specific constraints:

        - Job listings must transparently indicate an ongoing labor dispute and mention that roles are replacements for striking or locked-out employees.

        - Employers are barred from hiring professional strikebreakers, individuals with a history of replacing workers during strikes or lockouts across multiple employers. Employing such individuals can have serious legal consequences.

4. Penalties for Hiring Professional Strikebreakers: Employing professional strikebreakers is not taken lightly. Errant employers and strikebreakers can face up to $1000 in fines, a maximum of 90 days in county jail, or both.

Concept Check Questions

1. Which federal form must employers maintain to verify employee eligibility to work in the U.S.?
   a) W-2
   b) I-9
   c) W-4
   d) 1040

2. When onboarding a new hire in California, which form is required to document their tax withholdings?
   a) W-2
   b) I-9
   c) W-4
   d) 1099

3. Which agency handles enforcement of the state's employment discrimination protections?
   a) Department of Labor
   b) Equal Employment Opportunity Commission
   c) Department of Fair Employment and Housing
   d) National Labor Relations Board

4. What is the maximum number of work hours allowed in a standard California workweek?
   a) 35 hours
   b) 40 hours
   c) 45 hours
   d) 50 hours

5. What is the maximum number of hours 14 and 15-year-olds may work in office and clerical jobs per week in California?
   a) 10 hours
   b) 16 hours
   c) 20 hours
   d) 40 hours

6. Which of the following violations would result in overtime pay under California labor laws?
   a) Working 7 hours in a day
   b) Working 50 hours in a week
   c) Working 9 hours on the 7th consecutive workday
   d) Working 10 hours with a 1-hour lunch break

7. What is the maximum number of hours 16 and 17-year-olds can work per week in California?
   a) 10 hours
   b) 20 hours
   c) 30 hours
   d) 48 hours

8. What is the maximum fine under California law for an employer's initial failure to provide required meal and rest breaks?
   a) $50
   b) $250
   c) $500
   d) $1000

9. What penalty can California employers face if a wage check bounces due to insufficient funds?
   a) One week lost wages
   b) Double lost wages
   c) Up to 30 days lost wages
   d) Triple lost wages

10. How frequently must California employers provide a notice detailing wage payment time and location?
    a) Yearly
    b) Monthly
    c) Weekly
    d) Ongoing

11. Within how many days must an employer register with California's EDD after paying $100 in wages?
    a) 7 days
    b) 10 days
    c) 15 days
    d) 30 days

12. Which California payroll tax helps fund the state's disability insurance program?
    a) ETT
    b) SDI
    c) UI
    d) FICA

13. What penalty may California employers face for late filing of 1099-MISC forms after August 1?
    a) $50
    b) $100
    c) $250
    d) $500

14. Which tax is California employers required to pay to fund workforce training programs?
    a) EITC
    b) FICA
    c) ETT
    d) SUTA

15. What reporting method must California employers use to submit tax returns and wage reports?
    a) Mail
    b) Fax
    c) Electronically
    d) Phone

16. What are California employers required to provide with each employee paycheck?
    a) Pay stub
    b) W-2
    c) 1099-MISC
    d) Exemption forms

17. Under California law, how long does an employer have to provide an employee's final wages if they quit without notice?
    a) Immediately
    b) 24 hours
    c) 48 hours
    d) 72 hours

18. How much paid time off must California employers allow for employees to vote on election day?
    a) 1 hour
    b) 2 hours
    c) 4 hours
    d) A full work day

19. Under California law, when must an employer pay out owed wages if they lay off an employee?
    a) On the next pay date
    b) Within 3 days
    c) Within a week
    d) Immediately

20. How many weeks of military caregiver leave are allowed under California law?
    a) 12 weeks
    b) 20 weeks
    c) 26 weeks
    d) 52 weeks

21. Which federal law protects veterans' reemployment rights after returning from service?
    a) USERRA
    b) ADA
    c) NLRA
    d) OSHA

22. What is the negotiated agreement between a union and employer called?
    a) Trade pact
    b) Bargaining contract
    c) Collective agreement
    d) Concession deal

23. What tactic involves employers preventing employee access to the workplace during a labor dispute?
    a) Strike
    b) Lockout
    c) Picketing
    d) Rally

24. What must employers disclose in job postings if hiring replacements during a strike?
    a) Nothing
    b) Low pay
    c) Dangerous conditions
    d) Ongoing labor dispute

Concept Check Solutions

1. B) I-9. Employers are required to maintain the federal I-9 forms, which verify employee eligibility to work in the United States. The W-2 documents wages, the W-4 is for tax withholding, and the 1040 is an individual tax return.

2. C) W-4. When onboarding a new hire in California, the federal W-4 form is required to document the employee's tax withholding allowances. It determines federal income tax deductions.

3. C) Department of Fair Employment and Housing. In California, the Department of Fair Employment and Housing handles enforcement of the state's laws and regulations prohibiting employment discrimination. The other entities operate at the federal level.

4. B) 40 hours. According to California's labor laws, the maximum number of work hours allowed in a standard workweek is 40 hours. Longer workweeks up to 45 or 50 hours may be permitted with employee agreements, but the baseline maximum is 40.

5. B) 16 hours. In California, minors 14-15 years old working in office and clerical roles have a weekly cap of 16 hours. The other options show incorrect values, as this age group can only work limited part-time hours.

6. C) Working 9 hours on the 7th consecutive workday. Under California labor law, working more than 8 hours on the 7th consecutive workday requires overtime pay at 1.5 times the regular rate. The other scenarios do not trigger overtime requirements.

7. D) 48 hours. In California, minors ages 16-17 have a weekly maximum of 48 work hours. The lower options of 10, 20, or 30 hours would be incorrect.

8. A) $50. Under California law, the maximum fine for an employer's initial failure to provide the required meal and rest breaks is $50. Higher amounts of $250, $500, and $1000 are incorrect.

9. C) Up to 30 days lost wages. Under California law, a bounced wage check due to insufficient funds can result in a penalty to the employer of up to 30 days additional lost wages. Less or more is not specified.

10. D) Ongoing. California employers must provide notice detailing the time and place of wage payments on an ongoing basis per the state labor code. Yearly, monthly, and weekly are insufficient.

11. C) 15 days. Under California law, employers must register with the state's EDD within 15 days after paying $100 or more in taxable wages. Shorter periods of 7 and 10 days are incorrect. 30 days would exceed the requirement.

12. B) SDI. The California State Disability Insurance (SDI) tax is deducted from employee wages to help fund the state's disability insurance program providing benefits when someone cannot work due to illness or injury. ETT, UI, and FICA are different types of taxes.

13. B) $100. Under California law, a $100 penalty applies to late filing of 1099-MISC forms by employers after August 1. Lower amounts of $50 and $250 are incorrect, as is $500 which only applies for unfiled returns.

14. C) ETT. California's Employment Training Tax (ETT) is paid by employers to help fund workforce training programs in the state. EITC, FICA, and SUTA are unrelated taxes.

15. C) Electronically. Under California law, employers must submit tax returns, wage reports, and deposits to the EDD electronically rather than by mail, fax, or phone.

16. A) Pay stub. California employers are required to provide a pay stub or statement with each employee paycheck detailing their gross pay, deductions, and net pay. W-2, 1099-MISC, and exemption forms are unrelated.

17. D) 72 hours. If an employee quits without providing notice, California employers have 72 hours to provide the final wages. Immediately, 24 hours, and 48 hours would not comply with the 72 hour allowance.

18. B) 2 hours. California employers must provide up to 2 hours of paid time off for employees to vote on election day if they lack adequate non-work time to vote. 1 hour, 4 hours, and a full day are incorrect.

19. D) Immediately. Under California law, if an employer decides to lay off an employee, any owed wages must be paid immediately at the time of termination. Other options allowing delayed payment do not comply.

20. C) 26 weeks. California law aligns with federal regulations allowing 26 weeks of military caregiver leave to care for a seriously ill or injured family member in the military.

21. A) USERRA. The Uniformed Services Employment and Reemployment Rights Act is the federal law that protects veterans by guaranteeing reemployment rights when returning from military service.

22. C) Collective bargaining agreement. The negotiated contract between a labor union and an employer is known as a collective bargaining agreement. Trade pact, bargaining contract, and concession deal are not accurate terms.

23. B) Lockout. A lockout is when employers prevent employee access to the workplace during a labor dispute. A strike is the opposite, and picketing/rallying are related actions.

24. D) Ongoing labor dispute. Job postings to hire replacements during a strike must disclose that roles are to replace striking workers and that there is an ongoing labor dispute, per federal law.

Insurance and Liens

Safeguarding Contractors: A Comprehensive Guide to Bonds and Licensing

This chapter provides an in-depth exploration of the essential protective measures available for contractors and business owners. From bonds to insurance policies, we'll cover mechanisms designed to ensure the security and smooth operation of contracting businesses.

Understanding Bonds in Contracting

For large-scale projects funded by banks, insurance companies, or other financial institutions, contractors often need to provide a bond. These bonds can be acquired from bonding companies and generally cost around 1-2% of the contract's total value. Contractors should account for this cost when bidding for projects.

Key Types of Bonds:

1. **Bid Bond:** Ensures that the contractor will adhere to the project's contractual terms. It also eliminates non-serious bidders and can bridge the cost gap if a contractor fails to deliver.

2. **Performance Bond:** Guarantees that the contractor will finalize the project as per the agreed-upon conditions.

3. **Payment Bond:** Assures that the contractor will settle payments with subcontractors and suppliers. This bond becomes mandatory for federal contracts exceeding $35,000.

4. **Fidelity Bond:** Shields business owners against employee-related fraud or theft.

Bond Requirements for Contractors in California:

1. **State License Board Contract Bond:** To acquire a license in California, contractors must first secure a contractor's license bond or cash deposit worth $25,000 with the Contractor's State License Board (CSLB). This bond provides compensation if the contractor defaults in payment or infringes on licensing laws.

2. **Bond of Qualifying Individual:** Separate from the primary contractor's bond, this $25,000 bond covers key personnel like Responsible Managing Employees or Officers. A waiver is possible if the responsible individual holds at least 10% of the company's voting stock.

3. **LLC Bond:** Limited Liability Companies (LLCs) need an additional $100,000 bond alongside the standard contractor's bond.

4. **Disciplinary Bond:** Essential for new or reissued licenses, especially if previous licenses were revoked due to violations. The bond's value varies based on the nature of the infraction and should remain valid for a minimum of two years.

Alternative Bonding Options:

Contractors can opt for alternatives to the standard surety bond when filing with the CSLB. Valid options include certificates of deposit, savings and loan investment certificates, cashier's checks, or U.S. government bonds. Note that volatile assets, such as stocks, aren't accepted.

Consequences of Bond Issues on Licensing:

If bonds are canceled, reduced, or if the contractor fails to maintain the required bond amount or deposit, a license may face suspension. However, it's possible to reinstate the suspended license by securing a new bond and submitting it to the CSLB within 90 days of its activation or the old bond's cancellation.

Contractor Insurance in California

Insurance is an essential safeguard for businesses, offering protection from unforeseen events like fires, thefts, or injuries. When a contractor opts for an insurance policy, they pay premiums, and in return, the insurer assumes certain risks. Importantly, unlike bond arrangements, insurance doesn't mandate policyholders to repay any claims the insurer fulfills. Project requirements often specify the types and extents of insurance a contractor must hold. While workers' compensation is the most prevalent, some assignments might necessitate other insurances, such as property or vehicle coverage.

California Workers' Compensation Insurance: A Closer Look

In California, employers are bound by law to avail workers' compensation insurance for their workforce. It covers every employee – from full-time to part-time workers, minors, and even family members working in the business. Distinguished as a no-fault insurance system, the state administers this plan which is procured by the employer. Its primary objectives are to:

1. Cap the employer's liability for compensations.

2. Deter expensive legal battles for benefits.

3. Guarantee prompt medical care and comprehensive benefits for work-related injuries.

Contractors, before receiving their license, must either:

1. Demonstrate proof of workers' compensation insurance.

2. Secure permission from the State Department of Industrial Relations to self-insure.

3. Declare they don't employ anyone and hence are exempt from workers' compensation mandates.

Once insured, contractors must share their insurer's details with the registrar of contractors within a three-month window. This information must also be visibly displayed at work sites, and every employee should have written knowledge of their rights to claim benefits.

Prime contractors bear the responsibility of ensuring subcontractors also maintain valid workers' compensation. If a subcontractor lapses in this duty, any injuries sustained by their workers could lead to the prime contractor's liability.

Benefits and Claim Process:

An injured worker has 30 days to report the injury in writing to their employer. Following this, the employer must:

1. Enlighten the worker about the statutory benefits.

2. Report the injury to their insurance provider within five days.

This insurance encompasses a suite of benefits, from medical care and job displacement to temporary and permanent disability benefits. In tragic cases of fatalities due to work injuries, the insurance extends death benefits to the deceased's dependents.

Beyond Workers' Compensation: Protecting Other Business Facets

Apart from workers' compensation, contractors can further shield their operations through diverse insurance types, such as:

1. Vehicle insurance

2. Property coverage

3. Inland marine insurance

4. Builder's risk insurance

5. General liability coverage

6. Employee health and life insurance

7. Key personnel insurance

8. Comprehensive (umbrella) insurance

Each insurance type is tailored to defend specific business elements, spanning from tangible assets like property and machinery to indispensable staff and overall operations.

Understanding Mechanic's Liens in California: Rights, Processes, and Remedies

A mechanic's lien is a legal tool allowing those who've contributed to a property's improvement (like contractors, subcontractors, suppliers, or laborers) to claim payment if they haven't been compensated for their work or materials. It's a claim against the property itself, akin to a mortgage, and it's documented at the county recorder's office. If the owed amount remains unpaid, the property could face foreclosure due to the lien.

Mechanic's Liens under California Law:

In California, if a contractor is left unpaid after completing a project, they can enforce payment using a mechanic's lien or even file a claim against the property they worked on. But, before initiating a mechanic's lien, the contractor must give a heads-up to the owner. This is done using what's known as a mechanic's lien warning. Notably, this warning is exempted for some contracts, especially those aligned with service and repair norms.

For the lien to be recognized, it must be registered against the property's title in the county recorder's office, where the property is located. This document should detail the owner's information, property address, work specifics, and the amount due. The process mirrors the recording of a home loan or second mortgage.

Filing and Enforcing a Mechanic's Lien:

It's essential to note that a mechanic's lien can lead to a foreclosure, culminating in the property's public auction. The funds obtained from this sale then settle the contractor's outstanding payments. However, these liens are specific. They can only be filed against the exact property where the unpaid work took place. Public properties are off-limits for such liens, but contractors have the alternative of a "stop notice" when dealing with public properties.

For a mechanic's lien to be set in motion:

1. The property and its owner must be accurately identified.

2. The owner should be aware of all completed or ongoing work.

3. The lien needs to be registered within 90 days of completing the work.

Just registering the lien doesn't guarantee payment. Contractors must additionally file a lawsuit to uphold the lien within 90 days of its registration. This action preserves the lien's validity until there's a resolution – either payment is done, or the lawsuit concludes.

How Can Property Owners Respond?

Owners can extricate their property from a lien by offering a lien release bond, which is typically 125% of the claimed lien amount. This bond safeguards against potential lien claims, ensuring the property isn't mired in legal disputes. With this bond in place, owners regain the freedom to sell or further develop their property.

Completion and Cessation Notices

Understanding Completion Notices:

A completion notice is a formal written document verified by the property owner or their agent. It highlights the project's completion date, owner's details, property identification, and the original contractor's name (if there was one for the specific portion of the project). The goal of this notice is to condense the time frame for filing a lien.

Typically, there's a 90-day window to file a lien. However, once a completion notice is filed with the county recorder's office, this window shrinks to 60 days for prime contractors and 30 days for suppliers or subcontractors. The catch is that this notice should be filed within 15 days after completing the contract. Furthermore, it's pertinent to understand that a single completion notice caters only to one contractor. So, if multiple contractors are involved in a project, each one needs its separate notice.

What is a Cessation Notice?

A cessation notice shares some similarities with the completion notice. This formal document, filed by the property owner at the county recorder's office, signifies the end of work on a property. For such a notice to be valid, the property should have no work performed for a preceding 30-day period before the notice is recorded, with no intention of resuming work.

Once this notice is in place, the timeframe for filing a lien is adjusted to 60 days for prime contractors and 30 days for suppliers or subcontractors. However, there's a relief for smaller residential property owners: if the property houses four or fewer units, owners aren't obligated to provide either a completion or cessation notice.

Understanding the Preliminary Notice and Its Implications for Property Owners and Contractors

The Preliminary Notice Explained:

A preliminary notice is a protective legal tool meant to keep property owners informed about any ongoing work on their property. This can be issued by subcontractors or suppliers either to the property owner or to a construction lender, based on the scenario. When a tenant or the owner's representative hires a prime contractor, it is the contractor's duty to notify the owner through this notice.

For the process to be effective, there are time constraints: the notice must be given within 20 days after the labor or materials start being provided. After it's issued, the property owner has a 10-day window to acknowledge its receipt.

Who Should Issue the Notice and What Should It Contain?

Subcontractors required to give out a preliminary notice usually fit into specific categories:

1. Those whose contracts amount to $400 or more.

2. Those who liaise with tenants or architects rather than directly with the property owner.

3. Those involved in projects backed by construction loans.

4. Those working on public works initiatives.

The notice isn't just a casual letter. It must be detailed, encompassing:

- The name and address of the person offering the labor/materials.

- A total price estimate.

- An overview of labor, materials, or services provided or due to be provided.

- Contractor or subcontractor details.

- A clear description of the job site.

- An assertion from the claimant about their right to potentially file a mechanic's lien if left unpaid.

- If a construction lender is part of the equation, the contract's full price should also be mentioned.

For the delivery, the notice can be sent via certified or registered mail, with a return receipt. Or, it can be personally handed over. An essential step is to complete a proof of notice declaration, a verified record of the notice's delivery, handy during disputes.

Although optional, contractors can file this preliminary notice with the county recorder's office. This ensures they get alerted if any cessation or completion notice related to the contract gets filed.

Owner's Rights and Responsibilities:

Owners have the right to push back against a preliminary notice by lodging a notice of non-responsibility. This action becomes relevant if an owner has either received a preliminary notice or finds out about work commissioned without their consent. To be effective, the owner should file this notice within 10 days of being aware. This document, prominently displayed at the work site, liberates the owner from contractor payment liabilities, blocking any potential mechanic's lien from being filed by the involved parties.

Furthermore, when settling payments, owners can ask for either a conditional or an unconditional release from the parties involved. While a conditional release specifies certain conditions to be met prior to releasing the lien, an unconditional release clears the property from any mechanic's lien, irrespective of conditions being met or not. Once such an unconditional release is handed over, it prevents any future mechanic's lien from being lodged against the property.

The Stop Notice: A Mechanism to Secure Payment in Construction Projects

The stop notice serves as a way to secure funds in construction projects, much like a mechanic's lien is used to secure a claim against property. For contractors who've completed their tasks but haven't been compensated by the prime contractor, the stop notice becomes a crucial tool. By filing this notice, they request that the property owner, construction lender, or public entity reserve the necessary funds to fulfill the claim.

Distinguishing Stop Notices from Stop Orders:

It's essential to differentiate between a stop notice and a stop order. While a stop notice focuses on securing unpaid funds, a stop order mandates halting work on a project due to legal infractions, like the absence of workers' compensation.

Stop Notices in Public Property Context:

When working on public properties, contractors can't leverage the mechanic's lien. In such scenarios, the stop notice becomes their sole mechanism to pursue unpaid amounts. However, there's a catch: prime contractors in public works projects can't issue a stop notice to the awarding body. Only suppliers or subcontractors have that privilege.

What to Include in a Stop Notice:

A comprehensive stop notice should contain:

- Contractor's name, address, and signature.

- The recipient of the provided services.

- Detailed descriptions of the work, materials, and equipment used.

- An estimation of the work's worth.

- The overall contract amount.

For a stop notice to culminate its course, a lawsuit should be initiated between 10 and 90 days from the notice's issuance date.

Bond Requirements and Implications:

Stop Notice Bond: In contracts that involve a construction lender, the issuance of a valid stop notice requires a stop notice bond. This bond, valued at 125% of the claimed amount, ensures payment to all parties if the stop notice claim doesn't hold up. Note: public works projects are exempt from needing a stop notice bond.

Stop Notice Release Bond: If the contractor seeks the release of funds held by the stop notice, a release bond – again, 125% of the stop notice amount – must be posted. If the stop notice claim is upheld, the aggrieved party will draw from the release bond, instead of the initially secured funds.

Concept Check Questions

1. What is the minimum duration a disciplinary bond must remain valid after issuance in California?
   a) 1 year
   b) 18 months
   c) 2 years
   d) 3 years

2. What bond helps protect against employee theft for contractors?
   a) License bond
   b) Performance bond
   c) Fidelity bond
   d) Financial security bond

3. What is the penalty if a contractor fails to maintain an active license bond in California?
   a) License revocation
   b) Fine up to $1000
   c) Possible license suspension
   d) Jail time

4. Which workers' compensation insurance requirement applies to prime contractors regarding subcontractors in California?
   a) Providing coverage
   b) Verifying coverage
   c) Reporting injuries
   d) Managing claims

5. Which type of insurance protects contractors against losses from employee theft or embezzlement?
   a) Liability insurance
   b) Property insurance
   c) Fidelity bonding
   d) Worker's compensation

6. What legal document allows contractors to claim payment if they are unpaid for work done?
   a) Mechanic's lien
   b) Stop payment notice
   c) Labor claim
   d) Payment bond

7. What is the time limit for registering a mechanic's lien after completing work in California?
   a) 30 days
   b) 60 days
   c) 90 days
   d) 120 days

8. What is the alternate option contractors can use to claim payment against public properties?
    a) Stop notice
    b) Legal injunction
    c) Labor complaint
    d) County lien

9. What is the potential consequence if a registered mechanic's lien remains unpaid?
    a) Property foreclosure
    b) Contractor fines
    c) Owner bankruptcy
    d) Court hearings

10. What is the purpose of a completion notice under California law?
    a) To verify project approval
    b) To shorten lien filing timeframes
    c) To initiate final inspections
    d) To transfer property ownership

11. How soon must a completion notice be filed after finishing work on a project?
    a) 7 days
    b) 10 days
    c) 15 days
    d) 30 days

12. What is the purpose of a preliminary notice for contractors in California?
    a) To initiate inspections
    b) To verify project approval
    c) To inform property owners of work being done
    d) To transfer liability

13. Which contractors are mandated to send preliminary notices for public works projects?
    a) Prime contractors
    b) Subcontractors
    c) Suppliers
    d) Laborers

14. How can a property owner prevent liability for unauthorized work done?
    a) Lien release bond
    b) Stop work order
    c) Notice of non-responsibility
    d) Conditional release

15. When is the latest a subcontractor can send a preliminary notice after starting work?
    a) 10 days
    b) 15 days
    c) 20 days
    d) 30 days

16. Which party must send a preliminary notice if a tenant hires a contractor?
    a) Tenant
    b) Contractor
    c) Supplier
    d) Owner

17. Who can file a stop notice against a public entity for a public works project?
    a) Prime contractor
    b) Subcontractor
    c) Supplier
    d) Laborer

18. Which document is required to legally issue a stop notice with a construction lender?
    a) Permit copy
    b) Contract copy
    c) Stop notice bond
    d) Notice of completion

19. What is the typical required value of a stop notice release bond in California?
    a) 100% of claim amount
    b) 125% of claim amount
    c) 150% of claim amount
    d) Double the claim amount

20. Who has the right to issue a stop notice against a private property owner in California?
    a) Prime contractor only
    b) Prime and subcontractors
    c) Suppliers only
    d) Laborers only

Concept Check Solutions

1. C) 2 years. In California, a disciplinary bond issued to a contractor must remain valid for a minimum duration of 2 years after being acquired. Shorter periods of 1 year or 18 months would not comply.

2. C) Fidelity bond. A fidelity bond serves to protect employers against potential employee theft or fraud. License, performance, and financial security bonds have different applications.

3. C) Possible license suspension. If a contractor fails to maintain an active license bond or sufficient deposit in California, their license may face suspension as a penalty. Revocation, fines, or jail time do not apply.

4. B) Verifying coverage. Prime contractors in California carry the responsibility of verifying that any subcontractors they use also maintain active workers' compensation insurance. Providing coverage, reporting injuries, and managing claims are not the prime's duties.

5. C) Fidelity bonding. Fidelity bonds specifically protect employers against losses due to employee theft, embezzlement, or fraud. Other insurances and workers' compensation do not cover such risks.

6. A) Mechanic's lien. A mechanic's lien is the legal document that allows contractors, subcontractors, suppliers etc. to claim payment if they are unpaid for work done on a property. Stop notices, labor claims, and bonds do not serve this exact purpose.

7. C) 90 days. Under California law, a contractor has 90 days after completing work to register a mechanic's lien against the property. Shorter periods of 30 or 60 days would not comply with the legal timeframe.

8. A) Stop notice. On public properties where mechanics liens are not applicable, contractors can file a stop notice to claim unpaid dues in California. Injunctions, complaints, or county liens would not apply.

9. A) Property foreclosure. If a registered mechanic's lien in California goes unpaid, the potential consequence is the property facing foreclosure and being sold at a public auction. Other options do not directly apply.

10. B) To shorten lien filing timeframes. The purpose of a completion notice under California law is to condense the timeline that contractors have to file a mechanic's lien after finishing work on a property. It does not verify approval, initiate inspections, or transfer ownership.

11. C) 15 days. Under California law, a completion notice must be filed within 15 days of finishing work on a project in order to shorten lien filing timeframes. Shorter periods of 7 or 10 days, and 30 days, do not comply.

12. C) To inform property owners of work being done. The purpose of a preliminary notice in California is to keep property owners informed about any ongoing work on their property that they may be liable to pay for. It does not initiate inspections, verify approval, or transfer liability in itself.

13. B) Subcontractors. In California, subcontractors are specifically required to send preliminary notices for public works projects they are involved in. Prime contractors, suppliers, and laborers do not have this mandate.

14. C) Notice of non-responsibility. If unauthorized work is done, California property owners can file a notice of non-responsibility within 10 days to avoid liability for paying contractors. Other options do not achieve this.

15. C) 20 days. In California, the latest a subcontractor can send a preliminary notice after starting work is 20 days. Shorter periods of 10 or 15 days, and longer 30 days, do not comply.

16. B) Contractor. If a tenant hires a contractor for work on a California property, it is the contractor's duty to send the preliminary notice to inform the owner. Tenant, supplier, and owner do not have this responsibility.

17. B) Subcontractor. On public works projects in California, only subcontractors and suppliers can file a stop notice against the public entity to secure unpaid funds. Prime contractors and laborers cannot file stop notices.

18. C) Stop notice bond. For California contracts with a construction lender, a valid stop notice requires a stop notice bond valued at 125% of the claim. Permit, contract copies, and completion notices are not mandatory.

19. B) 125% of claim amount. In California, a typical stop notice release bond must be valued at 125% of the amount of the claim. 100%, 150%, or double the claim value are incorrect.

20. B) Prime and subcontractors. Against a private property owner in California, both prime contractors and subcontractors have the right to issue stop notices for unpaid funds. Suppliers and laborers cannot.

Contract Requirements and Execution

Mastering the Art of Construction Bidding: Strategies, Pitfalls, and Best Practices

The cornerstone of a contractor's profession lies in the precision of estimating and bidding. While an overbid might cost them an opportunity, an underbid could mean financial catastrophe. This chapter shines a spotlight on the intricacies of bid formulation, including the vital costs to consider, the diverse array of construction contracts, and the options to navigate when contracts go awry.

What is Bidding?

At its core, bidding is a competition where individuals or businesses put forth their best price for a service or product. The potency of a contractor's proposal hinges on their bid. This competitive contract bidding often unfolds publicly, inviting contractors to vie for the top spot. The process encompasses soliciting sealed bids and eventually crowning the most qualified low bidder. Various factors, like material costs, labor, and other variables, shape the final bid.

The Importance of Accurate Bidding:

For contractors, profitability is paramount. Accepting a job that doesn't guarantee profit jeopardizes their business longevity. It's paramount to grasp that no legal safety net exists to protect a contractor from the ramifications of an ill-considered bid stemming from flawed estimates. If they've agreed to a misjudged job, they're bound to honor it. Hence, astute estimation, which encompasses direct and overhead costs and ensures a profit, is essential.

Dissecting Bid Calculations:

Bid estimates encompass various terms:

- **Direct Costs**: This includes wages, materials, equipment, permits, and fees.

- **Overhead Costs**: Encompassing costs like office supplies, advertising, bad debts, and storage. Fixed costs, like office rent, are constants, whereas variable costs, such as utility bills, may vary.

After tallying all these expenses, a bid should be poised to generate a profit, typically ranging between 10 to 15%, though this can differ based on individual business parameters.

Bidding Mistakes to Avoid:

Errors in the bidding process range from hasty estimates due to lackluster planning, vague plans and specifications, misunderstanding the project's scope, overreaching the company's capacity, or bidding driven by competition instead of project value. Diligent planning, encompassing labor, material costs, overhead, profit margins, and the contractor's financing approach, is pivotal to sidestep these blunders.

Commitment to the Bid:

Once a bid is greenlit, contractors are legally bound to uphold the contract's stipulations. Overlooked items or unforeseen problems don't warrant charging more than the agreed bid. Altering the original price is only permissible if the client strays from the contract's terms. Hence, meticulous checklists and scrutiny of their estimations can be invaluable for contractors.

Final Considerations Before Bid Submission:

Before presenting their bid proposal, contractors should rigorously review all elements, from drawings, material samples, to product data, ensuring every requirement is meticulously met. This entails timely delivery and sometimes sealed bids even for private projects, underscoring the essence of fairness and integrity in the process.

Cost Management in Projects: Labor Costs and Aligning Budgets

Cost management is an essential business practice where the actual costs of a project are juxtaposed with its initial estimates. When actual costs surpass the budgeted ones, it's imperative to introduce strategies to curtail expenses and manage costs adeptly.

Understanding Labor Costs:

Labor costs usually make up the lion's share of a project's total expense. These encompass hourly wages, payroll taxes, health benefits, insurance outlays, and vacation allowances. A meticulous calculation of these costs is imperative, factoring in the different work classifications. It's worth mentioning that any wage settlement disputes can also skew these figures.

Several inefficiencies, like wasted materials, unproductive downtime, unwarranted overtime, and frequent employee turnover, can inflate total costs. To mitigate these, contractors need robust strategies to rein in labor costs. By ensuring an optimal use of the workforce, these strategies aim to achieve top-notch results at reduced costs. Measures can encompass comprehensive planning, astute scheduling, effective timekeeping, prudent inventory handling, and recruiting and training the right talent.

Classifying Labor Costs:

Labor costs can be bifurcated into direct and indirect categories:

- **Direct Labor Costs**: These are the costs for workers who are hands-on with a project. Although these can be pre-estimated, the eventual costs hinge on the time the job takes.

- **Indirect Labor Costs**: These pertain to workers who, while playing supportive roles, aren't directly immersed in the project itself.

Tools and Challenges in Cost Management:

Managing costs entails an arsenal of tools and methodologies. A gamut of factors can sway costs during a project's span, affecting the financial inflow and outflow. Among these challenges are unforeseen delays, inflated costs, and alterations in orders and their associated expenses. Given the unpredictable nature of these factors, cost management typically leans on meticulous plans drafted during the project's inception.

Outcomes of Effective Cost Management:

The primary goal of cost management is to initiate corrective actions to sync the project's execution with its blueprint. If there's a misalignment, the cost forecasts need revisiting. Keeping the project owner in the loop about any revisions is pivotal, as these can ripple out to impact other facets of the project roadmap.

Understanding Contracts: Types, Elements, and Methods

A contract is a legally enforceable agreement made between two or more entities, be they individuals or businesses. It represents a promise or series of promises that can be upheld in a court of law. Contracts come in three primary forms: implied, verbal, and written.

Types of Contracts:

1. **Implied Contract:** This arises from the behavior of the parties rather than explicit communication. It inherently trusts that the work will meet acceptable standards, the materials will be of commendable quality, and the contractor will receive just payment.

2. **Verbal Contract:** This is a spoken agreement, not documented. Suitable for minor tasks, verbal contracts can be challenging to enforce in legal disputes compared to written contracts.

3. **Written Contract:** A detailed document specifying the obligations and responsibilities of all parties. It offers a clear roadmap of what is expected and serves as concrete evidence in legal cases. If a verbal agreement transitions to a written one, only the latter is admissible in court.

Essential Elements of a Valid Contract:

For a contract to be legally binding, it should embody:

- **Offer and Acceptance:** A contractor typically proposes a bid. The client has the options to accept, decline, or negotiate the terms. Acceptances should mirror the original bid without deviations.

- **Consideration:** This pertains to the reciprocal exchange of value or services. For example, a client provides the contractor with access to a property for a renovation project in exchange for the contractor's expertise and labor.

- **Legality:** Every contract should align with existing laws. An illegal contract is null and void.

Contracts exceeding $500 must be documented. However, having all contracts, irrespective of value, in written form ensures clarity of roles and eases enforcement. This rationale explains why jobs over $500 necessitate a contractor's license. For contracts below $500, a verbal agreement suffices unless both parties opt for a written one.

If a contractor collaborates with a supposed owner, the contract must clearly indicate the actual property owners. When a contract is signed with an owner's representative, that person should confirm their legal accountability for payment.

Methods of Contracting:

1. **Single Prime Contracting:** Here, the owner employs one firm to handle the entire project. This company may engage subcontractors. A notable variant of this is the turnkey model where the contractor also sources the project's financing and land. While the owner might engage other professionals like architects or managers, only one bid is accepted.

2. **Multiple Prime Contracting:** Different project aspects (like framing or plumbing) are awarded to individual contractors. This decentralizes management for the owner but can be cost-effective due to multiple bids and the absence of subcontractor markups.

Essentials of Home Improvement Contracts in California

A home improvement contract serves as a legal commitment between a contractor and either a property owner, a tenant, or a home improvement salesperson. Such contracts encompass alterations made not just to a home's main structure, but also to its exterior and adjacent structures. This means that besides modifications inside the house, the contract can cover repairs, additions, and enhancements like driveways, swimming pools, terraces, landscaping, basements, and more.

Key Provisions in the Contract:

For clarity and transparency, a home improvement contract should:

- Detail all labor, services, and materials involved.

- Clearly specify the initial down payment amount.

In California, the California State License Board (CSLB) regulates the down payment amount to be either $1000 or 10% of the total contract price, whichever is lower. Notably, contractors possessing a blanket performance and payment bond can bypass this restriction, allowing them to ask for heftier initial payments.

Progress Payments and Joint Checks:

Following the down payment, contractors are allowed to bill for progress payments. These can be levied for either materials or labor, but only post the delivery of materials to the site or the completion of the respective work.

To ensure payment reaches subcontractors or material suppliers, property owners have the option of using a joint check. This is addressed to both the primary contractor and the third party, ensuring both parties receive their dues.

Protection for Contractors:

The mechanic's lien law safeguards contractors against non-payment by owners without valid reasons. Should an owner refuse payment without cause, a contractor can leverage this law to file a lien on the worked property, providing a security layer against unjust payment refusals.

However, there's a crucial caveat for contractors in California. Those without a valid license lack this protection. Consequently, property owners bear no legal obligation to pay unlicensed contractors, even with a signed agreement. This highlights the critical nature of contractors securing the appropriate licensing before taking on home improvement tasks.

Understanding the Three-Day Right to Cancel Home Improvement Contracts

Homeowners' Rights and Protection:

State laws are in place to champion homeowners' rights, enabling them to terminate home improvement contracts without any penalties. This protection is aimed at preventing undue pressure from aggressive sales methods and in-home salespeople. Sellers must provide homeowners with a set period during which they can reflect on the proposed purchase. Until this period ends, contractors are limited to only preliminary tasks like obtaining building permits.

Laws Governing the Right to Cancel:

The three-day cancellation privilege is primarily outlined under two acts: the Home Solicitation Act and the Federal Truth and Lending Act. Specifically:

1. **The Home Solicitation Sales Act** allows homeowners to cancel any deal exceeding $25 made at their residence or away from the contractor's main business location within three days of contract signing.

2. **The Federal Truth and Lending Act** (covered in Business and Professions Codes 7163, 7100, and 63) deems a contract unenforceable when a contractor assists with financing or loan arrangements unless all involved parties agree, and the three-day cancellation period concludes.

Cancellation Process:

To exercise the right to cancel, homeowners must send the contractor written notice expressing their choice not to proceed with the contract. This notice, ideally in a 12-point boldface font, should state:

"Three-Day Right to Cancel: As the buyer, you can terminate this contract within three business days. To do so, send a written notice via email, mail, fax, or direct delivery to the contractor's business address before midnight of the third business day after receiving a dated and signed contract copy containing this notice. Please include your name, address, and the date of receiving the contract."

Upon cancellation, the contractor is obligated to refund any payments within ten days. The homeowner should ensure any delivered goods under the contract remain at their residence in their original condition. If the contractor doesn't retrieve these goods within 20 days post-cancellation, the homeowner can retain them without any obligation. Conversely, if the homeowner doesn't make these goods available or return them, they're still bound by the contract's terms.

The contract itself should incorporate a checkbox in a 12-point boldface font which reads: "The law mandates the contractor provides a notice detailing your right to cancel. If you've received this notice, please initial the checkbox."

Limitations:

It's vital to note this cancellation right is exclusive to contracts negotiated away from the contractor's primary business location.

Post-Disaster Contractual Provisions and Protections

The Seven-Day Right to Cancel Following a Disaster:

When a disaster such as a fire, earthquake, or riot leads to a state of emergency declaration by the President or the Governor, homeowners benefit from a unique seven-day right to cancel post-disaster home repair contracts. This provision ensures that, alongside any signed repair contract addressing disaster damage, homeowners receive a seven-day cancellation notice. To cancel, homeowners can send an email, mail, or deliver a written notice within this period.

Upon contract cancellation:

- The contractor must refund any received payments.

- The homeowner should return any materials provided by the contractor within ten days. If these materials are not collected by the contractor within 20 days of the cancellation, the homeowner has the right to retain them.

Pricing and Penalties Post-Disaster:

For 180 days after a disaster declaration, contractors cannot charge over 10% above their standard rates (as per Penal Code 396) for services. Exceptions exist if higher labor or material costs justify the price increase. Breaching Penal Code 396 can lead to a year in county jail, a $10,000 fine, or both. This is also recognized as an unfair business practice under the California Business and Professions Code, possibly incurring further civil penalties.

Warranties and Contractor Liability:

Any warranty provided by a contractor must be in writing, detailing the work covered, duration, and any manufacturer warranties for materials or appliances used. The CSLB allows a four-year period for consumers to report issues with a project. If the contract includes extended warranties, this deadline may be extended. Contractors can face liability for:

- Patent defects (visible errors with a four-year liability).

- Latent defects (structural issues with a ten-year liability).

Per the BNP Code 702 8 D, the CSLB can probe unlicensed contractors for up to four years from the date of any illegal act.

Payments and Retention:

Retention, or retainage, refers to a part of the contract's price held by the owner until project completion. This sum is paid to contractors or subcontractors once the project receives final approval. Contractually, retention amounts should be transparent. It's common for primary contractors to withhold around 10% (similar to their subcontractors) from progress payments.

A final payment request encompasses the final payment sum and any retentions due. This payment is processed post the final project inspection, owner's approval, and necessary documentation submission.

Lastly, contracts should contain details about work commencement, defining what is meant by "substantial commencement of work." It should notify that if a contractor doesn't begin significant work within 20 days from the agreed start date, without a valid reason, it's a breach of the contractor's licensing laws.

Guidelines for Service and Repair Contracts in Residential Settings

Understanding Service and Repair Contracts:

Service and repair contracts are tailored for specific scenarios. They apply when:

1. The contract amount is $750 or less.

2. The buyer contacts the contractor for the specific work.

3. The contractor only offers services essential for the buyer's initial concern.

4. Payment is made after the completion of work.

If a residential remodeling contract doesn't fit these criteria, it should be classified as a home improvement or swimming pool contract.

Key Features of Service and Repair Contracts:

Upon starting the job with a fully signed, legitimate contract, the right to cancel for the buyer becomes void. While these contracts bear resemblances to standard home improvement contracts, they possess distinct attributes:

- **Parts Replacement:** Contractors must offer customers any replaced parts during service. If customers opt not to keep these parts, they can mark the box titled "OK for contractor to take replaced parts."

- **Service Charges:** If there's a service fee, it must be clearly itemized under the "Amount of Service Charge" heading. The contract should state that only one such fee, encompassing any trip or inspection costs, can be charged.

- **Cancellation Rights:** The contractor must inform the customer that their cancellation rights cease once the work starts. This advisory, in 12 point boldface type or larger, should be attached to the contract, and the buyer must date and sign it.

Mandatory Contractual Inclusions:

The contractor's license law prescribes specific inclusions:

- The text should be in a minimum of 10 point typeface with headings in 10 point boldface unless stated otherwise by the Business and Professions Code.

- Contractors with two or more license suspensions or revocations within eight years must disclose such actions if the work involves residential properties of four units or fewer.

- Contracts for owner-occupied, single-family homes must highlight policies on extra work and change orders.

- Contracts demanding general liability insurance and workers' compensation should annex disclosure attachments.

- Every contract needs a mechanic's lien warning, elucidating the rights and duties of both the owner and the contractor concerning this warning.

Key Elements of Construction Contracts: Provisions, Responsibilities, and Liens

Understanding Contract Provisions:

Contract provisions play a pivotal role in ensuring clarity and mutual understanding among involved parties. These clauses detail essential aspects like pricing, payment modalities, responsibilities of involved parties, special conditions, and the protocols for addressing contract breaches.

Roles and Responsibilities:

1. **Contractor's Duties:** The contractor usually has a multi-faceted role, which includes:

   - Obtaining relevant licenses and building permits.

   - Procuring and delivering necessary materials.

   - Providing labor and managing the workforce.

   - Ensuring adherence to local codes and regulations.

   - Completing tasks as per the agreed blueprint and guidelines.

   - Keeping the construction site tidy.

2. **Owner's Duties:** The property owner is generally tasked with:

   - Prompt approval of designs and blueprints.

   - Ensuring the property aligns with zoning regulations.

   - Timely payments as per the contract.

   - Covering costs related to permits and other official charges.

   - Offering essential property descriptions and surveys.

   - Allowing the contractor uninterrupted access to the work site.

Supplemental Conditions and Pricing Details:

Supplemental conditions, which are customized to suit individual projects, provide additional terms that modify the contract's general conditions. These conditions can delve into specific project protocols, legal stipulations, and insurance requirements.

Price determination and payment terms are integral to contracts. The pricing methodology could adopt various formats: lump sum, cost-plus, unit price, or a guaranteed maximum cost. All costs, from the total project price to any down payments and other charges, should be detailed clearly.

Progress Payments and Federal Regulations:

Progress payments are incremental payments made upon the achievement of certain construction milestones. Typically, these payments cover 90% of the work, retaining 10% until the project's completion.

The Federal Prompt Payment Act ensures that contractors involved in federal projects are paid promptly. Delays in payment attract interest penalties. Prime contractors should receive their dues within 14 days of invoicing, and they, in turn, must pay subcontractors within seven days of receiving their payment.

Liens – A Safety Net for Contractors:

Liens act as a safeguard for those owed money for labor or materials in property enhancement. They restrict the property owner from selling without settling the dues. If payments remain unsettled, a court might authorize a property sale, using the proceeds to clear the debt.

Understanding Contract Breaches: Material vs. Immaterial Violations

A breach of contract, commonly known as a contract violation, arises when a party—be it the owner or the contractor—fails to uphold their responsibilities as stipulated in the contract. This could manifest as outright refusal to perform, conducting actions in contradiction to the contract's terms, or hindering another party from executing their duties. Such breaches can be broadly categorized into two types: material breaches and immaterial breaches.

1. Material Breach:

A material breach denotes a grave failure to adhere to the terms and conditions of the contract, compromising the essence of the agreement. For instance:

- A contractor delivering substandard materials or workmanship.

- An owner changing project specifications without proper adjustments or consents.

Consequences of a material breach can be stringent. Typically, it culminates in the termination of the contract and can escalate to legal battles. Should a lawsuit ensue, the wronged party might receive compensation for their losses. This compensation, often labeled as "liquidated" or "stated" damages, might already be defined within the contract.

Timeliness is also critical. Even in the absence of a defined completion timeline in the contract, the onus is on the contractor to wrap up the project promptly. Unwarranted delays could make the contractor liable for damages due to loss of use. Sometimes, contracts dictate a daily penalty for such delays. As an illustration, if the contract charges a penalty of $300 per day and the project overshoots by 50 days, the contractor would face $15,000 in liquidated damages. Importantly, if an owner seeks liquidated damages, they forfeit the right to claim actual damages for the same violation.

It's crucial to initiate any lawsuit for a breach within a stipulated timeframe. Missing this window could mean permanently forfeiting the right to press charges.

2. Immaterial Breach:

An immaterial breach, often termed a partial breach, pertains to minor deviations from the contract, which don't dismantle the foundational agreement. In such scenarios, the affected party can only claim damages equivalent to the actual loss incurred due to the breach.

Navigating Contractual Disputes: A Guide to Courts and Litigation Procedures

The Landscape of Contractual Litigation:

A significant breach of contract often culminates in litigation. Many of these disputes that wind their way to the courts are centered on three core aspects:

1. Establishing the validity of a contract.

2. Pinpointing the material damage borne by either the owner or contractor due to non-fulfillment of contract terms or unpaid dues.

3. Determining and awarding the appropriate damages.

The Superior Court:

The Superior Court, commonly referred to as the trial court, stands as the primary judicial arena where cases are evaluated. Here, a judge (and sometimes a jury) hears testimonies and reviews evidence to deliver a verdict. This court oversees both small claims and more expansive civil cases. It's imperative for contractors to notify the Contractors State License Board (CSLB) of any verdicts from this court within a 90-day window. Should the defendant choose to appeal, the case then moves to the appellate court.

Small Claims Court:

Operating under the county court umbrella, the Small Claims Court is tailored for prompt and economical dispute resolution without the involvement of attorneys. Disputes here might span property damage, personal injury, breach of agreements, fraud, and more. While individuals can lodge claims up to $10,000, businesses have a ceiling of $5,000. However, individuals are restricted to only two claims that surpass $2,500 annually. All such claims get processed at the county clerk's office.

For those contemplating a lawsuit, it's crucial to be mindful of the Statute of Limitations, which sets the time frame for lodging a claim. This window usually oscillates between 2 to 4 years post the event, contingent on the nature of the claim. But, if the target of the lawsuit is a government or public agency, the claim must be lodged within a truncated span of just six months.

Limited and Unlimited Civil Lawsuits:

If one wishes to be legally represented, they can opt for a limited civil lawsuit in the superior court rather than the small claims court. These suits, encapsulating amounts up to $25,000, come with steeper fees and need to adhere to all protocols of a regular civil case. Though they offer more comprehensive legal procedures, they also require longer durations—possibly a year—to reach a resolution, compared to the speedier three-month trajectory in small claims. If one seeks legal guidance without actual courtroom representation, this is termed "limited scope representation."

For disputes involving sums north of $25,000, the procedure transitions to what's known as unlimited civil cases. The protocols and filing procedures for these mirror those of limited civil lawsuits.

Understanding Arbitration: An Alternative to Lawsuits in Construction Disputes

Arbitration offers a quicker alternative to traditional lawsuits. It employs a neutral third party, which can be a solo arbitrator or a panel, to resolve disputes. Importantly, there are arbitrators who possess expertise in construction-related issues.

Initiating the Process:

The arbitration journey begins when the plaintiff, the party initiating the complaint, communicates their intent to arbitrate. This notice can be directed to the Contractors State License Board (CSLB) or the opposing party (defendant). It's crucial for both sides to agree to arbitration. Arbitration can either be binding, where the decision is final and cannot be contested in court, or non-binding, where either party can seek a trial if they disagree with the arbitration outcome. Notably, the CSLB exclusively offers binding arbitration.

CSLB Arbitration Programs:

The CSLB has two free arbitration services for contractors with a clean record:

1. **Mandatory Arbitration:** This avenue is selected when a plaintiff desires the CSLB to tackle a complaint for cases below $15,000. Both parties' presence is mandatory. If the provided form isn't returned by the plaintiff within 30 days, the complaint might be dismissed. On the flip side, if the respondent neglects the 30-day form submission window, the arbitration continues in their absence.

2. **Voluntary Arbitration:** Suited for disputes ranging between $15,000 and $65,000, this option is pursued when both parties are willing. Non-compliance in returning the CSLB-provided form within 30 days by either party may lead to complaint closure. In both these CSLB arbitration formats, parties have the liberty to engage legal counsel or self-represent. A key aspect to bear in mind is the binding nature of the arbitrator's decision. Any non-compliance with the given verdict within 30 days might result in the contractor's license being revoked.

Private Arbitration:

There's also the realm of private arbitration, which operates outside the CSLB purview. Here, both parties jointly decide on the arbitrator. It's essential for contractors to communicate the outcomes of such private arbitration endeavors to the CSLB in written form within a 90-day frame; failing which they may face a potential license suspension.

Concept Check Questions

1. What is an underbid risk that contractors should avoid?
   a) Excessive paperwork
   b) Financial losses
   c) Low profit margins
   d) Project delays

2. When can a contractor legally raise their bid price above the original contract?
   a) After starting work
   b) If costs were underestimated
   c) If owner changes contract terms
   d) Due to price increases

3. Which factor does NOT impact a contractor's bid amount?
   a) Labor costs
   b) Profit margins
   c) Bonding rates
   d) Overhead expenses

4. How can contractors reduce ineffective labor costs?
   a) Using subcontractors
   b) Providing training
   c) Increasing wages
   d) Reducing crew size

5. What is a common challenge of construction cost management?
   a) Excess materials
   b) Permit delays
   c) Order changes
   d) Equipment failure

6. Which cost factors may still vary after estimating direct labor expenses?
   a) Payroll taxes
   b) Health benefits
   c) Hours worked
   d) Hourly wages

7. What minimum contract value requires a written agreement for contractors in California?
   a) $200
   b) $400
   c) $500
   d) $1000

8. Which element is NOT legally required in a binding contract?
   a) Offer and acceptance
   b) Consideration
   c) Collateral
   d) Legality

9. What clause should be included if the owner's agent signs a contract?
   a) Payment terms
   b) Work schedule
   c) Agent liability
   d) Permit requirements

10. When is an implied contract formed between a contractor and client?
    a) With a handshake agreement
    b) When work begins without written contract
    c) After completing a small project
    d) After bid is accepted

11. Which is an example of consideration in a contract?
    a) Bid invitation
    b) Performance bond
    c) Payment schedule
    d) Material specifications

12. What is the maximum down payment percentage allowed on home improvement contracts in California?
    a) 5%
    b) 10%
    c) 15%
    d) 20%

13. What is the purpose of a joint check for home improvement projects?
    a) Verify project completion
    b) Pay subcontractors
    c) Settle disputes
    d) Release liens

14. What is the timeframe for homeowners to cancel a home improvement contract in California?
    a) 24 hours
    b) 48 hours
    c) 3 days
    d) 5 days

15. What amount of time do contractors have to refund payments after a cancellation?
    a) 3 days
    b) 5 days
    c) 10 days
    d) 15 days

16. When can a contractor begin full project work after signing a contract at a residence?
    a) After 3 days
    b) After permit is issued
    c) After down payment is made
    d) Immediately

17. What should homeowners do if contractors don't provide the cancellation notice?
    a) File a complaint
    b) Cancel within 5 days
    c) Withhold payment
    d) Continue the contract

18. How long is the contractor cancellation period for homeowners after a declared disaster?
    a) 3 days
    b) 5 days
    c) 7 days
    d) 10 days

19. What is the penalty for illegally overcharging following a disaster declaration?
    a) License suspension
    b) $10,000 fine
    c) 1 year in jail
    d) Combination of fine and jail

20. For how long can homeowners report issues with disaster repair work?
    a) 2 years
    b) 4 years
    c) 6 years
    d) 10 years

21. What payment can contractors withhold until project completion?
    a) Down payment
    b) Progress payments
    c) Retention
    d) Final payment

22. When must contractors provide homeowners warranty details?
    a) At contract signing
    b) After starting work
    c) Upon request
    d) At project completion

23. How long can the CSLB investigate unlicensed contractors for illegal acts?
    a) 2 years
    b) 4 years
    c) 6 years
    d) 8 years

24. When does a customer lose the right to cancel a repair/service contract?
    a) After 3 days
    b) After starting work
    c) After first payment
    d) Never

25. When must contractors disclose past license suspensions for repair/service contracts?
    a) Always
    b) For commercial projects
    c) For residential projects under 4 units
    d) Only upon request

26. How many service fees can contractors charge for repair/service contracts?
    a) None allowed
    b) One maximum
    c) Two maximum
    d) No limit

27. When must extra work policies be highlighted in repair contracts?
    a) All contracts
    b) Commercial projects
    c) Homeowner-occupied homes
    d) Rental properties

28. Which disclosure is required for contracts mandating liability insurance?
    a) Workers' compensation
    b) Project timeline
    c) Payment schedule
    d) Material suppliers

29. What is a contractor typically responsible for obtaining before starting work?
    a) Business license
    b) Building permits
    c) Material deposits
    d) Property surveys

30. What is an example of a supplemental contract condition?
    a) Payment amounts
    b) Work schedule
    c) Noise restrictions
    d) Quality standards

31. Who sets prompt payment deadlines under the Federal Prompt Payment Act?
    a) Property owners
    b) Prime contractors
    c) The federal government
    d) Subcontractors

32. What right is protected by liens filed against a property?
    a) Building access
    b) Final payment
    c) Material ownership
    d) Compensation owed

33. What type of breach involves a contractor stopping work mid-project?
    a) Immaterial breach
    b) Material breach
    c) Partial breach
    d) Minor breach

34. What is one consequence of a contractor's unwarranted project delays?
    a) Accelerated timeline
    b) Lowered payment
    c) Liquidated damages
    d) Material return

35. When can an owner NOT claim liquidated damages from a contractor?
    a) If actual damages are also sought
    b) If delay length is not defined
    c) If project scope changes midway
    d) If breach wasn't material

36. Which court hears contractor-owner contract disputes as a trial court?
    a) Small claims court
    b) Superior court
    c) County court
    d) Appellate court

37. How many claims over $2,500 can an individual file annually in Small Claims Court?
    a) None allowed
    b) 1 claim
    c) 2 claims
    d) 3 claims

38. Which court handles claims seeking over $25,000 in damages?
    a) Small Claims Court
    b) Superior Court
    c) Appellate Court
    d) County Court

39. Where are Small Claims Court cases first filed?
    a) Superior Court
    b) County clerk's office
    c) CSLB office
    d) State appeals office

40. Who makes the final decision in binding arbitration?
    a) Judge
    b) Jury
    c) Arbitrator
    d) Mediator

41. What happens if the plaintiff misses the CSLB arbitration form deadline?
    a) Case dismissed
    b) Defendant pays fees
    c) New deadline issued
    d) Case proceeds anyway

Concept Check Solutions

1. B) Financial losses. An underbid that is too low can result in the contractor taking financial losses on the project if their actual costs exceed the bid amount. Excess paperwork, low profits, and delays may occur but losses are the prime risk.

2. C) If owner changes contract terms. Contractors can only legally raise a bid price above the original contract amount if the property owner changes the terms of the contract after signing. Otherwise they must honor the original bid.

3. C) Bonding rates. Factors like labor, profit, and overhead impact a contractor's bid amount. Bonding rates do not affect the actual project costs and bid calculation.

4. B) Providing training. Providing adequate workforce training helps contractors reduce ineffective labor costs like wasted materials or unproductive downtime. Using subcontractors, increasing wages, or reducing crew size do not directly address inefficiencies.

5. C) Order changes. A common challenge in construction cost management is client order changes, which alter expenses. Excess materials, permits, and equipment failure are not direct challenges.

6. C) Hours worked. While direct labor hourly wages are estimated upfront, factors like overtime hours worked may still vary and exceed initial budgeting during a project. Taxes and benefits can be precisely determined.

7. C) $500. In California, contracts exceeding $500 between a contractor and client are required to be in written form. Lower thresholds of $200, $400, or $1000 do not align with the regulated amount.

8. C) Collateral. The essential elements that make a contract legally binding include offer/acceptance, consideration, and legality. Collateral, like a down payment or deposit, is not a mandatory component for a basic enforceable contract.

9. C) Agent liability. If a contract is signed by the owner's authorized representative or agent, it should include a clause confirming the agent's liability for making payments. Work schedule, permits, and payment terms do not address agency.

10. B) When work begins without written contract. An implied contract is formed when a contractor starts work without having a written contract in place, establishing an unspoken agreement. Handshakes, small projects, or bid acceptance do not qualify.

11. C) Payment schedule. A payment schedule outlining client compensation for the contractor's work is an example of consideration in a contract. Bid invitations, bonds, and material specifications do not represent consideration.

12. B) 10%. For home improvement contracts in California, the maximum down payment that can be collected is either $1000 or 10% of the total contract price, whichever is lower. Higher limits of 15% or 20% would exceed state regulations.

13. B) Pay subcontractors. The purpose of a joint check in home improvement projects is to pay subcontractors and material suppliers directly. It does not verify completion, settle disputes, or release liens.

14. C) 3 days. Under California law, homeowners have 3 calendar days to cancel a home improvement contract after signing. Shorter periods of 24 or 48 hours, or longer ones like 5 days, do not comply.

15. C) 10 days. Contractors have 10 calendar days to refund any payments made after receiving a valid cancellation notice from the homeowner. Shorter 3-5 day periods or longer 15 day ones do not comply.

16. B) After permit is issued. After signing a home contract at a residence, California contractors can only begin full project work after permits are issued, not immediately. Waiting 3 days or for payment does not apply.

17. A) File a complaint. If a cancellation notice is not provided in a California home improvement contract, homeowners should file a complaint against the noncompliant contractor. Withholding payment and continuing the contract are ill-advised.

18. C) 7 days. Following a declared disaster in California, homeowners have a 7-day right to cancel repair contracts. Shorter 3-5 day periods or longer 10 day ones do not apply.

19. D) Combination of fine and jail. The penalty for illegally overcharging after a California disaster declaration is up to a $10,000 fine and/or up to 1 year in county jail. License suspension is not applicable.

20. B) 4 years. Homeowners can report issues with California disaster repair work to the CSLB for up to 4 years from project completion. Shorter 2-year or longer 6-10 year periods do not apply.

21. C) Retention. Contractors typically withhold a retention amount from progress payments until project completion. Down payments, progress payments, and final payments are not withheld.

22. A) At contract signing. In California, contractors must provide homeowners warranty details in writing at the time of contract signing, not after starting work or on request.

23. B) 4 years. The CSLB can investigate unlicensed contractors for illegal acts for up to 4 years from the date of violation in California. Shorter 2-year or longer 6-8 year periods are incorrect.

24. B) After starting work. For California service/repair contracts, the customer's right to cancel ceases once the contractor begins the actual repair work as outlined in the agreement. Waiting 3 days, making the first payment, or never losing the right to cancel do not apply.

25. C) For residential projects under 4 units. Contractors in California must disclose past license suspensions/revocations in service contracts for owner-occupied, single-family residential projects under 4 units. This does not universally apply or only for commercial projects.

26. B) One maximum. Only one service fee can be charged by contractors for California service/repair contracts, encompassing all trip and inspection costs. Multiple fees or unlimited fees are prohibited.

27. C) Homeowner-occupied homes. For owner-occupied, single-family residential service contracts in California, extra work policies must be prominently highlighted. This is not a universal or commercial-specific requirement.

28. A) Workers' compensation. California repair/service contracts mandating general liability insurance must also include a workers' compensation disclosure attachment. Project timelines, payment schedules, and material suppliers are not applicable.

29. B) Building permits. Contractors are typically responsible for obtaining relevant building permits before commencing work on a project. Business licenses, material deposits, and property surveys are not their duty.

30. C) Noise restrictions. Supplemental contract conditions often cover special project-specific terms like restricting noisy work to certain times. Payment amounts, schedules, and standards relate to general, not supplemental conditions.

31. C) The federal government. Under the Federal Prompt Payment Act, the federal government sets standards for prompt payment timeframes that contractors on government projects must adhere to. Owners, prime contractors, and subcontractors do not set these regulations.

32. D) Compensation owed. Liens filed against a property aim to protect the right to receive compensation owed for labor, materials, or other enhancements to the property. Access, payment timing, and material ownership are not protected.

33. B) Material breach. A contractor stopping ongoing project work halfway through would be considered a material breach of the contract, severely violating the agreement's essence. Immaterial, partial, and minor breaches do not denote grave noncompliance.

34. C) Liquidated damages. If a contractor's unwarranted delays extend the project timeline, the owner can charge liquidated damages as compensation for loss of use. Lowered payment, accelerated timeline, and material return are not applicable.

35. A) If actual damages are also sought. Owners cannot claim pre-defined liquidated damages if they also try claiming actual losses for the same material breach. Liquidated damages are still applicable if delay length, project scope change, or breach level are uncertain.

36. B) Superior court. The Superior Court serves as the primary trial court venue that hears and judges contract disputes between contractors and clients in California. Small claims, county, and appellate courts do not hold trials.

37. C) 2 claims. Individuals in California are restricted to only 2 Small Claims Court filings exceeding $2,500 annually. Filing no, 1, or 3 high-value claims does not comply with state limits.

38. B) Superior Court. In California, unlimited civil lawsuits with over $25,000 in disputed damages must be filed in Superior Court. Small claims, appellate, and county courts have lower jurisdictional limits.

39. B) County clerk's office. To initiate a case, Small Claims Court filings are first submitted at the county clerk's office in California, not superior, CSLB, or appeals offices.

40. C) Arbitrator. In binding arbitration, the neutral third-party arbitrator makes the final case decision that must be adhered to. Judges, juries, and mediators do not decide outcomes in arbitration.

41. A) Case dismissed. If the plaintiff misses the 30-day form deadline in CSLB arbitration, the complaint may be dismissed or closed. Defendant fee payment, new deadlines, or case continuation regardless do not occur.

Public Works
Public Works Contracts and Contractor Requirements in California

Public works contracts involve tasks related to construction, alteration, demolition, installation, and repair, financed either fully or in part by public funds. These projects span various levels of government, from federal to local municipalities. Public works contractors, who undertake these projects, ensure that their employees are paid a prevailing wage.

Requirements for Registration with the Department of Industrial Relations (DIR)

Contractors wishing to be recognized as public works contractors by the DIR must fulfill several criteria:

1. Maintain workers' compensation for all staff.

2. Hold valid registration as a public works contractor, especially if acting as a subcontractor.

3. Possess a license from the Contractor State License Board (CLB).

4. Clear all wage-related dues or penalties owed to employees or regulatory bodies.

5. Ensure they are not barred from participating in bids or projects by any federal or state entity.

6. Adhere to registration norms and, in case of any violation, remain eligible for re-registration by covering any additional penalties.

For both registration and its renewal, contractors can visit the DIR website, pay the non-refundable fee, and complete the process online. Regardless of when the registration occurs, it remains valid from July 1st to June 30th each fiscal year.

Locating and Bidding on Public Works Projects

Prospective contractors can identify potential public works projects on city websites or through California's consolidated platform, Cal eProcure. This state-managed system allows contractors to seek out suitable projects based on specific parameters.

In California, it's a legal mandate for public bodies to invite open bids for select contracts, predominantly those in construction. To ensure a transparent process, these entities call for sealed bids and usually award the project to the most competitive bidder. The Subletting and Subcontracting Fair Practices Act, colloquially known as the Listing Law, is in place to deter malpractices like bid shopping and bid rigging.

Prequalification for Bidding

Certain public entities might require contractors to undergo a prequalification phase before placing their bids. This can pertain to an individual project or can be applicable to all bids within a year. Whenever public bodies set up such prequalification mechanisms, they must institute a consistent approach, a scoring method, and a process for appeals.

Contractor Bidding and Compliance in California Public Works Projects

Bidding requirements are essential for contractors to understand. Public entities often require contractors to provide a bid security when submitting their bids. This security, payable to the contract-awarding body, can range from $100 to $250 or up to 10% of the bid price, and 20% for federal contracts. The bid security can be in the form of a bid bond, cash, cashier's check, or certified check. If a contractor fails to provide the required bid security, their bid is deemed non-responsive and is rejected. The bid security serves as a guarantee that the bidder will honor the contract as per their submitted bid. If they fail to do so, the bid security is forfeited to the public entity.

For state public works projects valued over $5000, or other public works projects valued over $25,000, the bidder must file two surety bonds with the public entity awarding the contract before work commences. As per the Miller Act, federal government projects over $100,000 require a bid bond. These performance and payment bonds assure the contractor's ability to complete the awarded job. The bond must equal 100% of the contract value. The performance bond guarantees timely and satisfactory completion of the contract, while the payment bond ensures full payment for all materials and subcontract labor. The payment bond must be maintained until the end of the warranty period. The contractor is responsible for all bond premiums, costs, and incidentals, typically 1 to 2% of the contract value, based on the contract size and contractor's credit score.

In California, public entities must specify the required contractor's license classification in posted notices inviting bids. The awarding public entity must verify the contractor's license before awarding the contract. This verification can be done through the contractor, state license board, or by checking the contractor's pocket license along with a relevant signed statement by the contractor. Additionally, all public works contracts must include minority disability business solicitation requirements.

The listing law requires public works contractors to list their subcontractors by name, office location, and contractor license number at the time of bidding. These subcontractors will handle contract work valued at more than 0.5% of the prime contractor's bid or $10,000 or more for roadwork, whichever is greater. If the prime contractor does not identify the portion of contract work performed by each subcontractor, it is assumed that the prime contractor will perform those portions of work themselves. Substituting subcontractors without the approval of the awarding public entity is prohibited. Substitution can occur under certain circumstances such as failure to execute, insolvency, failure to perform, failure to furnish bonds, clerical error, unlicensed subcontractor, failure to pay prevailing wages, or if the subcontractor is not qualified.

If a prime contractor requests a substitution of a listed subcontractor, the public entity must provide written notice to the listed subcontractor of the prime contractor's request and reasons for the request by certified mail. The listed subcontractor has five working days to submit written objections to the substitution. If objections are submitted, a hearing will be held, and the public entity must provide written notice of the hearing to the listed subcontractor at least five working days before the hearing. At the hearing, the public entity will decide whether to consent to the prime contractor's request for substitution.

If a prime contractor violates the listing law, the public entity may cancel its contract with the prime contractor or assess a penalty of up to 10% of the amount of the subcontract involved. The prime contractor may also face disciplinary action by the Contractor's State License Board (CSLB).

Guidelines for Contractors in Public Works Projects

Understanding Prevailing Wages

Prevailing wages represent the standard hourly compensation, inclusive of benefits and overtime, given to laborers on public works projects worth more than $1,000. The Department of Industrial Relations (DIR) establishes these rates to maintain fairness across projects. Contractors must legally adhere to these rates when bidding on public works initiatives. These rates vary depending on the nature of the job and prevailing wages in the local labor market.

Exceptions exist. For instance, the project-awarding authority can initiate a Labor Compliance Program (LCP). Under this, prevailing wages might not apply to public projects up to $15,000 for tasks like demolition, maintenance, or repair, and $25,000 for construction. Additionally, the Davis Bacon Act mandates similar wage rates for workers on federal public works projects exceeding $2,000.

Liability Insurance Requirements

Public entities usually expect both contractors and subcontractors to showcase proof of liability insurance, naming the public entity as an extra insured party. This insurance should remain active before and during the contract's entirety. Detailed minimum insurance requirements for these projects can be consulted in the Law and Business Manual Table 8.1. Alongside this, proof of workers' compensation for all staff should be presented to the public body before finalizing the contract.

Warranty Provisions in Construction

Warranties are pivotal in construction contracts, and they come in two forms: expressed and implied. An expressed warranty generally lasts a year from the date the construction is substantially completed. But this doesn't hold for defective construction, seen as a contract breach. Such breaches have a four-year statute of limitations.

Withdrawing a Bid

At times, a contractor might wish to retract their bid. They can formally request the awarding public entity to pull back their bid before the final submission deadline. Contractors can resubmit after one withdrawal, as long as it's done before the deadline. Post the opening of bids, a contractor can withdraw their bid without surrendering their bid security in cases of specific errors, but only if the awarding entity allows. If the entity declines, the contractor has the right to pursue the return of their bid security without incurring additional costs or interest.

Competitive Bidding Process

In California, public works contracts are typically awarded through a transparent competitive bidding process. The primary goal of this system is to maintain fairness, avert favoritism, and prevent corrupt practices. Contractors present their bids in sealed envelopes to a specified office by an established deadline. On a predetermined date, these bids are unveiled and assessed. The reviewing period generally lasts a minimum of 20 business days unless otherwise specified. The contract eventually goes to the contractor who offers the lowest, most responsive bid. It's essential to note that non-registered contractors, if found bidding on or acquiring a public works project, might incur a penalty of $2,000.

Apprenticeship Mandates

For public works contracts priced at $30,000 or higher, both contractors and subcontractors must employ apprentices affiliated with the Division of Apprenticeship Standards (DAS). However, this obligation doesn't extend to professions or trades that don't engage apprentices. Penalties for flouting these stipulations can be stringent. Initial infringements might lead to a fine of $100 per day of violation. Any subsequent violations within three years escalate this fine to $300 per day. Furthermore, the offending contractor might be debarred for a duration ranging from one to three years, depending on the number of infractions. Debarment implies a contractor's loss of rights to bid or be granted a public works contract or to function as a subcontractor on a public works assignment.

Certified Payroll Reporting

Besides employing the California DIR electronic system for certified payroll reporting, most public works contractors and subcontractors are obliged to submit their certified payroll records (CPRs) to the Labor Commissioner. These detailed records should catalog essential information like each employee's personal and employment details, hours worked, and wages earned. However, projects overseen by a Labor Compliance Program (LCP) are exempted from this online reporting requirement to the DIR.

Potential Violations and Consequences

Several potential pitfalls await contractors in the realm of public works contracts. These include falsely categorizing workers, underreporting hours, neglecting to report all workers, soliciting wage kickbacks, and not providing due fringe benefits. The repercussions of such violations can be severe, ranging from financial penalties and owed wage settlements to criminal charges and reimbursement of the DIR's investigative expenses.

Concept Check Questions

1. What registration is required for public works contractors in California?
   a) DIR registration
   b) CSLB license
   c) OSHA certification
   d) EPA permit

2. Where can contractors find public works bid opportunities?
   a) DIR website
   b) Cal eProcure
   c) City websites
   d) All of the above

3. How are bids typically submitted for public works projects?
   a) Email
   b) Online form
   c) Sealed bid
   d) Open bid

4. What must exist for prequalification mechanisms?
   a) Scoring method
   b) Appeal process
   c) Consistent approach
   d) All of the above

5. What is the most common form of bid security for public works?
   a) Bid bond
   b) Certified check
   c) Cashier's check
   d) Cash

6. What do performance and payment bonds guarantee on public works?
   a) Timely completion and labor/materials payment
   b) Warranties and legal compliance
   c) Future bonding and final payment
   d) Lowest bid and quality workmanship

7. When must contractors list subcontractors and their license numbers?
   a) After being awarded contract
   b) At time of bidding
   c) After starting work
   d) Only upon request

8. How must a prime contractor notify a listed sub of substitution request?
    a) Email
    b) Phone
    c) Certified mail
    d) No requirement

9. When must prime contractors prove license classification for public bids?
    a) After award
    b) During bidding
    c) At contract signing
    d) Pre-qualification

10. What is the minimum contract value requiring prevailing wage payment?
    a) $500
    b) $1,000
    c) $5,000
    d) $10,000

11. When must contractors show proof of public works liability insurance?
    a) During bidding
    b) Before contract signing
    c) Before and during contract
    d) Only upon request

12. What is the goal of competitive sealed bidding for public works?
    a) Transparency
    b) Favoritism
    c) Speed
    d) Limited competition

13. How long is the minimum review period for public bids?
    a) 10 days
    b) 15 days
    c) 20 days
    d) 30 days

14. What is the penalty for an unregistered contractor bidding on public works?
    a) License revocation
    b) $2,000 fine
    c) 5 year bidding ban
    d) Misdemeanor

15. What can skirt online CPR reporting to the DIR?
     a) Subcontractors
     b) Projects under $100,000
     c) Labor Compliance Program
     d) Federally funded projects

Concept Check Solutions

1. A) DIR registration. To be recognized as public works contractors in California, companies must register with the Department of Industrial Relations (DIR). CSLB licensing, OSHA certification, and EPA permits do not apply.

2. D) All of the above. Contractors can locate California public works bid opportunities on city government websites, the state's Cal eProcure site, or other consolidated platforms that compile listings. No single source is used exclusively.

3. C) Sealed bid. To ensure transparent bidding, public entities in California mandate sealed bid submissions for public works contracts that meet monetary thresholds. Email, online forms, and open bids are not required protocol.

4. D) All of the above. Public contractor prequalification mechanisms instituted by California public entities must include consistent criteria, a scoring methodology, and a process for appeals and evaluating them. Not just one single component is mandatory.

5. A) Bid bond. The most common form of bid security required for public works bids is a bid bond, which guarantees the bidder will honor their submitted bid if awarded the contract. Certified checks, cashier's checks, and cash are less prevalent options.

6. A) Timely completion and labor/materials payment. On public works, performance and payment bonds guarantee satisfactory and timely project completion as well as full compensation for all labor and materials, respectively. Warranties, legal compliance, future bonding, final payment, low bids, and quality workmanship are not guaranteed.

7. B) At time of bidding. Under California's Listing Law, prime contractors must list all subcontractors, their locations, and license numbers when submitting public works bids, not after contract award or starting work. Post-award listing is prohibited.

8. C) Certified mail. Prime public works contractors in California must notify listed subcontractors of any substitution requests via certified mail per state law. Email, phone, and no notification do not meet requirements.

9. B) During bidding. Public entities in California must require bidders to prove their proper license classification for the type of public works contract during the bidding process before awarding the contract. This is not done after award or contract signing.

10. B) $1,000. In California, public works contracts valued at more than $1,000 require prevailing wage payment to laborers. Lower $500 thresholds or higher $5,000 and $10,000 ones do not trigger prevailing wage mandates.

11. C) Before and during contract. For California public works, contractors must provide proof of liability insurance naming the public entity as additional insured before contract signing and maintain it throughout the contract duration. Only upon request or selective timing do not comply.

12. A) Transparency. Competitive sealed bidding for public works aims primarily to ensure transparency, fairness, and avoidance of favoritism or corruption in the contract award process. It does not seek to limit competition or speed.

13. C) 20 days. California requires a minimum 20 business day review period for evaluating public works bids after opening, unless otherwise stipulated. Shorter 10-15 day or longer 30 day minimums do not comply.

14. B) $2,000 fine. If an unregistered contractor in California bids on or obtains a public works contract, they risk a $2,000 penalty. License revocation, bidding bans, and misdemeanors are not applicable penalties.

15. C) Labor Compliance Program. Projects monitored under a public entity's Labor Compliance Program (LCP) are exempt from mandated online certified payroll reporting to the DIR system. Subcontractors, project values, and funding sources do not impact CPR reporting requirements.

Safety

OSHA and Cal/OSHA: Ensuring Workplace Safety in the U.S.

The 1970 establishment of the Occupational Safety and Health Act, commonly known as OSHA, marked a landmark move in enhancing workplace safety across the U.S. The act's mission is simple: to cut down workplace-related injuries, illnesses, and deaths. Thanks to its efforts, work-related deaths decreased by 60%, and injuries fell by 40%. OSHA's main duties include enforcing safety guidelines, providing training, and collaborating with other programs for enhanced safety.

Who Does OSHA Cover? While OSHA encompasses most private sector employers and workers, it doesn't cover self-employed individuals and certain federal agencies with unique safety standards. Interestingly, religious entities employing people for non-religious tasks (like maintenance) are under OSHA's watch.

State-Level Safety Initiatives: While OSHA sets the baseline, 26 states, with California included, have curated their safety and health programs. OSHA supervises these programs, and if a federal rule is stricter or covers an area the state doesn't, the state must adjust accordingly within six months.

The Cal/OSHA Framework: In California, workplace safety operates under Cal/OSHA, referencing standards in Title 8 of the California Code of Regulations. Compared to the federal guidelines, Cal/OSHA has additional requirements like illness prevention programs, stringent communication about hazards, and strict exposure limits to harmful chemicals. In cases where a federal standard is missing but a state-level one exists, everyone should follow the state's rules.

Cal/OSHA's principles are enforced by California's Division of Occupational Safety and Health. Employers in California have specific obligations:

1. **Safety Programs:** Develop and maintain a program to prevent injuries and illnesses.

2. **Workplace Inspections:** Regularly inspect workspaces to pinpoint and rectify hazards.

3. **Tools and Equipment:** Ensure workers have and maintain safe tools and gear.

4. **Warnings:** Use signs, labels, color codes, or posters to notify workers of dangers.

5. **Medical and Training:** Offer medical checks and training as mandated by Cal/OSHA.

6. **Reporting:** Inform Cal/OSHA about any grave injury, illness, or employee death.

7. **Rights and Responsibilities:** Display the Cal/OSHA poster detailing workers' rights and responsibilities.

8. **Inspection Assistance:** Supply names of designated employee representatives to accompany Cal/OSHA during inspections.

9. **Citation Display:** If cited, exhibit the citation near the affected area until the issue is fixed or for at least three working days.

10. **Compliance:** Address violations by the deadline and submit necessary verification documents.

Employers are expected to uphold these standards to ensure a safe and healthy working environment for their employees.

OSHA Guidelines for Fall Protection in the Construction Industry

Falls stand as the predominant fatal risk in the construction domain, claiming an estimated 300 to 400 lives every year and leading to over 100,000 injuries. Recognizing this, OSHA has instituted specific guidelines to safeguard employees from falls and related dangers on construction sites.

When is Fall Protection Required? If there's a risk of a worker plummeting 6 feet or more to a level below, protection becomes mandatory. Such risks include unguarded edges, open sides, holes, construction areas with formwork, hoist zones, certain excavations, roofing tasks, wall openings, and specific masonry work, among others.

Modes of Fall Protection: Employers can employ a mix of measures to prevent falls:

1. **Guard Rails:** These are crucial for areas elevated 7.5 feet or more, such as balconies, porches, or any working spot 30 inches above the regular surface. Moreover, any wall opening with a drop exceeding 4 feet mandates guard rails. The rails should be robust, with top rails positioned 42 inches above the work level and mid rails or mesh filling the space to the floor. These railings must resist considerable force without yielding, ensuring the safety of workers.

2. **Safety Nets and Personal Fall Arrest Systems (PFAS):** Such systems need to surpass OSHA's stipulated standards and be regularly inspected by a certified professional.

3. **Barricades and Covers:** In scenarios where holes present a risk, covers that adhere to OSHA's standards are essential. These should be appropriately labeled and robust enough to handle double the weight of workers, equipment, and materials. Covers on roadways, however, should support twice the axle load of the heaviest vehicle anticipated.

4. **Warning Lines:** These ropes or chains, marked every 6 feet, surround roof work zones. They should withstand a 16-pound horizontal force and maintain stability when tugged.

5. **Hoisting Areas:** When not in operation, hoisting zones should have a chain gate or removable guard rail to prevent unauthorized access.

In a sector as risk-laden as construction, adhering to safety norms is paramount. OSHA's guidelines ensure that both employers and workers can create and operate within a safe environment, significantly reducing the chances of fatal accidents.

Guidelines for Personal Fall Arrest Systems

In the realm of construction, the potential for falls is an ever-present risk. Employing Personal Fall Arrest Systems (PFAS) is a critical step in safeguarding workers against such perils.

Understanding PFAS: A PFAS acts as a lifeline, designed meticulously to arrest a worker's fall midway. It encompasses several components:

A Personal Fall Arrest System Consists of 3 Main Components:
1. Full Body Harness
2. Connecting Device
3. Anchorage

1. **Body equipment**: Includes a belt or harness that the worker wears.

2. **Other components**: These can range from lanyards and lifelines to deceleration devices.

3. **Anchorage connector**: Secures the entire system.

Safety Standards for PFAS: For a PFAS to be effective, it should meet specific criteria:

- Cap the arresting force exerted on a worker wearing a harness to 1800 pounds.

- Restrict potential falls to no more than 6 feet, ensuring workers don't come into contact with levels below.

- Halt a worker's descent swiftly, with a maximum deceleration distance of 3.5 feet.

- Be robust enough to bear twice the force of a potential freefall.

Specifications for Lifelines and Lanyards: When leveraging safety belts, lifelines, and lanyards:

- Lifelines should anchor above the work point to a structure or anchorage that can bear at least 5000 pounds.

- Lifelines at risk of wear or cutting should be fortified, preferably with a minimum of 7/8-inch wire core manila rope.

- Safety belt lanyards, preferably crafted from half-inch nylon or an equivalent, should limit potential falls to 6 feet.

The Role of Safety Nets: For high-risk zones situated 25 feet or more above ground or water, and where conventional safety measures like ladders or scaffolds aren't feasible, safety nets become indispensable. Key guidelines include:

- Work initiation should post the installation and testing of safety nets.

- Nets should sprawl 8 feet beyond potential fall zones and be positioned as proximally beneath the work area as viable – but certainly not more than 30 feet below.

- In bridge projects, a single net level suffices.

- Nets should possess a mesh design no larger than six by six inches and should meet a minimum impact resistance standard of 17,500 foot-pounds.

The complexities of the construction domain make fall protection crucial. By adhering to these guidelines for PFAS and related safety measures, the industry can significantly diminish the inherent risks, ensuring worker safety remains paramount.

Scaffold Safety and Regulations

Scaffolding is fundamental to construction. Beyond its utility, understanding its regulations and safety protocols is paramount.

Permit Requirements:

In the US, scaffolding that exceeds three stories or 36 feet in height necessitates a permit. While steel and iron dominate scaffolding construction, various materials have their applications.

Safety Essentials:

- Scaffolds play a preventive role, averting accidents. Their use becomes essential when workers need a platform broader than 20 inches or a ladder.

- Only individuals with expertise and authority should handle scaffold assembly or disassembly.

- Scaffolds should have a dead load safety factor that allows them to carry their weight plus four times the intended working load. Working loads are classified by their weight capacity per square foot: light (25 lbs.), medium (50 lbs.), heavy (75 lbs.), and special-duty scaffolds. The capacity of special-duty scaffolds must be assessed by a qualified person or an experienced California-registered civil engineer.

Construction Guidelines:

- Ensure scaffolds are erected with precision: they should be plumb, level, and square.

- Manufacturer-provided railings are mandatory on work platforms elevated 7.5 feet or higher.

- Scaffolds with a height more than four times their base width need extra support or bracing.

- Scaffold planking should be robust, with a minimum thickness of two inches and a width of 10 inches.

- Fall protection is vital for scaffolds exceeding 10 feet in height. Dismantling should start from the top.

Types of Scaffolds:

1. **Supported Scaffolds:** Platforms held up by rigid beams or supports.

2. **Suspension Scaffolds:** Platforms suspended by non-rigid means from an overhead structure.

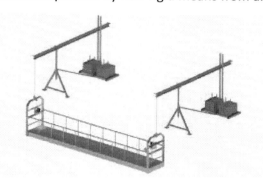

3. **Aerial Lifts:** Vehicle-mounted platforms like cherry pickers.

Popular scaffolds on sites include the fabricated frame, mobile, tube and clamp, two-point suspension, pump jack, ladder jack, and wood pole scaffolds.

Training and Prohibitions:

If an employee's proficiency in scaffold-related tasks is questionable, retraining is compulsory. OSHA prohibits certain scaffolding types, including unstable objects like loose tiles, bricks, stilts, or shore scaffolds.

Electrical Safety:
Although falls are the primary concern on scaffolds, electrocution isn't far behind. Adhering to clearance distances from power lines is vital. If near an insulated line under 300 volts, keep scaffolding at least 3 feet away. For uninsulated lines, the minimum distance is 10 feet.

Best Practices for Ladder Safety in Construction

Ladder safety is an indispensable component of construction. With various types and safety guidelines, understanding their proper use is vital.

Types of Ladders and Preliminary Steps:

The main ladders used in construction are step ladders and extension ladders. Prior to utilizing any ladder, always refer to the manufacturer's guidelines. It's imperative to abstain from ladder use if you're indisposed, medicated, or facing unfavorable weather.

Placement and Usage Guidelines:

- Always avoid placing ladders in high-traffic zones, especially doorways. If unavoidable, ensure doors are locked or have someone stand guard.

- When positioning a ladder, its feet should rest securely on the ground. For soft terrains, boards can provide added stability. Before climbing, always test the ladder's steadiness.

- Step ladders need to be fully extended and locked, while extension ladders should lean at a 75-degree angle against a supportive structure.

Safe Climbing Protocols:

- Ensure you, the ladder, and its rungs are dry. Ideally, another person should hold the ladder steady.

- Always maintain three contact points with the ladder. Climb with caution, centering your weight, and never overreach or use the topmost rungs.

Maintenance and Classification:

Ladders necessitate routine inspections for any signs of wear. Unfit ladders should be retired and labeled as hazardous. The job's nature dictates the ladder type; for example, for tasks requiring extended reach, extension ladders made of sturdy materials like aluminum are suitable.

Specific precautions include:

- Avoid using the pail shelf, top cap, or the adjacent step of a step ladder as standing or working points.

- Don't stand on the top three rungs of extension ladders without secure handholds or safety systems.

Ladders come with designated weight limits:

- Light-duty: 200 pounds

- Medium-duty: 225 pounds

- Heavy-duty: 250 pounds

- Extra heavy-duty: 300 pounds

- Special-duty: 375 pounds

Exceeding these can be hazardous; alternatives like scaffolding are more suitable.

LOAD CAPACITY*	DESCRIPTION	CSA CODE	ANSI CODE
200 lbs./91 kg	Household - Light Duty	Grade 3	Type III
225 lbs./102 kg	Tradesman and Farm - Medium Duty	Grade 2	Type II
250 lbs./113 kg	Construction and Industrial - Heavy Duty	Grade 1	Type I
300 lbs./136 kg	Construction and Industrial - Heavy Duty	Grade 1A	Type IA
375 lbs./170 kg	Construction and Industrial - Heavy Duty	Grade 1AA	Type IAA

*Includes user and materials

Ladder Length Restrictions:

Certain ladders have length constraints. For instance, step ladders shouldn't surpass 20 feet, two-section metal extension ladders 48 feet, and painter's step ladders 12 feet. Overlaps are mandated for two-section extension ladders: 36 inches for those up to 32 feet and 70 inches for 40-60 feet ladders.

Electrical Safety: Understanding Hazards and Precautionary Measures

Electrical safety is vital, especially when using temporary power sources like power tools, lighting, and pumps. With electrons flowing through such devices, the danger of electrocution amplifies. Awareness of potential electrical injuries, such as electrocution, electrical shock, burns, and indirect injuries, is essential for workplace safety.

Types of Electrical Injuries:

1. **Electrocution:** A lethal electrical shock that can result in burns, nerve damage, muscle contractions, cardiac arrest, paralysis, and sometimes death. It can inflict both internal and external injuries.

2. **Electrical Shock:** Occurs when a person becomes part of an electrical circuit, leading to varied severity based on the current's amount, path, duration, and frequency.

3. **Burns:** Electrical burns are due to heat from the electric current passing through the body. Burns can arise from electrical arcs or explosions (arc or flash burns) or by contact with overheated equipment (thermal contact burns).

4. **Indirect Injuries:** These injuries happen when an electrical shock's surprise element causes victims to fall or lose muscle function. Shocks above 2000 mA are particularly hazardous, with risks including cardiac arrest and severe burns.

Recognizing and Preventing Hazards:

Electrical safety starts with recognizing and controlling potential dangers. This entails pinpointing exposed electrical parts, damaged equipment, overloaded circuits, and improper grounding. De-energizing circuits before work is one effective prevention method.

Observable indicators of electrical hazards might include frequent tripping of circuit breakers, burning smells, unusually warm wiring, or damaged insulation.

Role of Ground Fault Circuit Interrupters (GFCIs):

GFCIs are invaluable in electrical hazard prevention. These tools detect ground faults, cutting off power in risky situations. Particularly useful in damp areas like bathrooms, they are mandatory for certain outlets not attached to a building's permanent wiring.

Safety Protocols and Inspections:

Regular equipment check-ups enhance safety. Misuse of electrical tools is dangerous and may result in OSHA penalties. Any damaged cords or wires must be labeled as non-functional and promptly replaced.

When handling power tools:

- Disconnect when not in use or during servicing.

- Avoid exposure to heat, oil, or sharp edges.

- Never carry tools by cords and avoid yanking them.

- Adhere to the tool's design limitations and use the appropriate protective gear.

Personal Protective Equipment

In the construction industry, Personal Protective Equipment (PPE) stands as a vital component in ensuring worker safety. All PPE, whether supplied by the worker or employer, must comply with the American National Standards Institute (ANSI) guidelines and gain the employer's nod.

The Role of PPE:

PPE acts as the last shield once other preventive measures are in place. This layered approach begins with engineering controls that adapt the work environment or machinery to diminish potential hazards. Safe work practices train employees to decrease their risk exposure. On the administrative front, controls relate to task management and scheduling to limit hazard exposure times.

From November 15, 2007, employers took on the responsibility of furnishing appropriate PPE at no extra cost to workers. They're also tasked with hazard identification, training on PPE usage and upkeep, and recording all PPE-related training. This curriculum spans the gamut from understanding PPE's importance to its lifespan and upkeep requirements.

Diverse PPE Categories:

1. **Head Protection:** Hard hats, a staple, should offer resistance against object penetration, impact shocks, and be water and flame-resistant. They're divided into:

    - Class A: Resists impacts and penetration, with limited electrical protection up to 2200 volts.

    - Class B: Offers maximal electrical safeguarding up to 20,000 volts, along with impact and penetration defense.

    - Class C: Prioritizes lightweight comfort sans electrical defense.

2. **Eye and Face Protection:** This can range from spectacles and goggles to specialized helmets and welding shields.

3. **Hearing Protection:** Mandatory when noise exposure crosses an 8-hour average of 90 decibels. A threshold of 85 decibels warrants a hearing conservation program encompassing exposure monitoring, training, and more.

4. **Hand and Arm Protection:** Depending on tasks, gloves guard against an array of dangers from abrasions to chemical burns. Crucially, asbestos in gloves is forbidden.

5. **Body Protection:** Workers exposed to severe temperatures, chemical hazards, or impact risks may don lab coats, vests, or even full-body suits, tailored from materials that counter specific threats.

6. **Foot and Leg Protection:** Necessitated when hazards like sharp objects, molten splashes, or electrical risks threaten. Protective footwear should resist impacts, endure heat, and, if for electrical tasks, be non-conductive. Maintenance is crucial for continued efficacy.

Fire Extinguishers: Types, Uses, and Safety Procedures

Fire extinguishers are indispensable safety instruments, each tailored for a specific type of fire. It's imperative to use them correctly, understanding their limits, especially for small, manageable fires.

Categorizing Fires:

Based on the fuel they consume, the National Fire Protection Agency (NFPA) classifies fires as:

- **Class A**: Ordinary combustibles like wood and paper.

- **Class B**: Flammable liquids and gases such as gasoline and propane.

- **Class C**: Electrical equipment fires.

- **Class D**: Combustibles like sodium and magnesium, which need specialized agents.

- **Class K**: Cooking oil and kitchen fires.

Choosing the Right Extinguisher:

Matching the fire to its respective extinguisher is paramount. The primary extinguishers include:

- **Water (APW)**: Suited for Class A fires.

- **Carbon Dioxide (CO2)**: Ideal for Class B and C fires.

- **Dry Chemical**: Suitable for Class A, B, and C fires.

- **Wet Chemical**: Designed for Class A, C, and K fires.

Safety and Operation Tips:

In emergent fire situations, always position yourself with an exit behind for a quick escape, bearing in mind that typical extinguishers last only 15-30 seconds. When using an extinguisher, follow the "PASS" method:

- **P**ull: Unlock the lever by pulling the pin.

- **A**im: Direct the nozzle toward the fire's base.

- **S**queeze: Hold the extinguisher upright and depress the trigger.

- **S**weep: Oscillate side to side, targeting the fire area. Reapply if the fire resurfaces.

Understanding the types of fires and their appropriate extinguishers can be life-saving. Always prioritize safety, and remember the PASS technique for effective fire mitigation.

Injury and Illness Prevention Program

Since 1991, every employer in California has been mandated to implement the Injury and Illness Prevention Program (IIPP), as described in Title 8, Section 3203 of the California Code of Regulations. Aimed at bolstering workplace safety and efficiency, this program stands as a testament to the state's commitment to employee wellbeing.

Cal/OSHA's Support:

Recognizing the challenges employers might face, the California Occupational Safety and Health Administration (Cal/OSHA) extends complimentary consultation services. These consultations, led by professionals, offer guidance in crafting an effective IIPP and provide pivotal health and safety training for both employers and employees.

Foundations of the IIPP:

- **Documentation and Leadership:** A comprehensive written IIPP is crucial, identifying designated competent individuals responsible for its execution. It's vital for the management to underscore its dedication to safety via robust organizational practices and measures to guarantee adherence to safety norms.

- **Communication:** Transparent communication lines must be established, ensuring employees are well-versed with safety norms. An open culture where employees can flag safety concerns without backlash is essential.

- **Safety Protocols:** The IIPP necessitates a written code of safe practices tailored to the contractor's scope of work. It should be easily accessible to all, especially supervisory personnel.

- **Risk Management:** A pivotal component is the systematic identification and management of potential risks. This encompasses routine inspections, thorough assessments of incidents, and maintaining comprehensive reports of any mishaps.

- **Equipment Operation and Safety Gear:** Only those with the requisite qualifications should handle heavy machinery. Additionally, whenever a task demands safety equipment, it's the contractor's duty to provide and ensure its optimal use.

- **Training:** Comprehensive training regimes, covering the gamut from recognizing risks to adhering to safety practices, are integral to the IIPP. This includes onboarding sessions for new employees, periodic safety meetings, and updated training when new equipment or processes are introduced.

Emergency Preparedness:

To deal with unforeseen incidents, the IIPP mandates that emergency medical provisions be in place. This translates to having a trained first-aid team on standby and ensuring that first aid kits are within easy reach.

Best Practices for Safe Excavation and Trenching

Excavation and trenching are common activities in the construction industry. However, they come with inherent risks, particularly when underground utilities are involved. To manage these risks in California, specific protocols, including engaging with the Underground Service Alert, are in place.

Engaging the Underground Service Alert:

Prior to any excavation or digging, it is a strict requirement to liaise with the Underground Service Alert. This free service, operational across California, plays a pivotal role in preventing damages. Once informed, their team will meticulously examine the excavation blueprint, flagging areas proximate to the proposed project. They delineate the positions of subterranean utilities, equipping both property owners and construction professionals with critical insights. It's imperative to contact them at least two days (and at most 14 days) prior to commencing the excavation. Neglecting to do so can lead to substantial penalties, ranging from $10,000 to a staggering $50,000 for intentional oversights. The team employs a system of concise, color-coded markers to differentiate each facility.

Trenching Protocols:

- **Spoil Piles:** When digging trenches, excess soil or 'spoil piles' must be kept a minimum of 2 feet away from the trench's periphery.

- **Ladder Requirements:** For trenches deeper than 4 feet, which workers will enter, ladders or ramps are obligatory. These must protrude 3 feet above the trench.

- **Shoring and Benching:** Trenches that extend beyond 5 feet in depth mandate the use of shoring and benching systems. For those surpassing 20 feet, a professional engineer must oversee the shoring design.

Soil Management and Excavation Protocols:

Soil sloping is an effective measure to avert excavation instability. The required ratios vary depending on soil type, with Type A at 0.75:1, Type B at 1:1, and Type C at 1.5:1. Excavations are exempted from these protocols if they are solely in rock, or are less than 5 feet deep, but only after a competent individual has confirmed the site's stability.

Shoring System Guidelines:

Implementing appropriate shoring techniques is paramount for trench safety. Standard systems involve:

- Solid wood sheeting (at least 2 inches thick).

- Plywood (1 1/8 inches thick minimum).

- Wood uprights (minimum 2 inches x 8 inches).

- Wood braces and diagonal shores (at least 4 inches x 4 inches).

A minimum of two braces is necessary for shoring trenches. Metal screw-type trench jacks, supplemented with a base or horizontal timber, are ideal. However, hydraulic jacks are also viable. In soils like clay, silt, or loam, shoring and bracing become vital. As trenches are left open, the likelihood of collapses increases. When dismantling shoring, start from the base, releasing jacks or braces progressively. In unstable terrains, ropes are recommended for extracting shoring materials.

Recording and Reporting Work-Related Injuries and Illnesses in California

Keeping Records:

California mandates employers to document work-related injuries and illnesses using Form 300. This form captures:

- All work-related deaths.

- Injuries or illnesses causing loss of consciousness, restrictions in work, job changes, absences, or medical care beyond basic first aid.

- Major injuries or illnesses diagnosed by a certified healthcare professional.

For every reported case, employers need to fill out an Injury and Illness Incident Report, either using Cal OSHA Form 301 or a similar format. If there's ambiguity about recording a case, employers should consult their regional Cal OSHA office.

Yearly Summaries and Accessibility:

For businesses with 11 or more workers, year-end data from Log 300 must be moved to Log 300A. This summary should be publicly displayed from February 1st to April 30th each year. Furthermore, employers have the obligation to:

- Allow current and former employees, as well as their representatives, access to the Log and Summary of Occupational Injuries and Illnesses (Cal OSHA Form 300).

- Grant employees or their authorized agents access to personal medical records and exposure details.

Reporting Serious Incidents:

In cases of severe injuries, illnesses, or fatalities:

- Employers must notify Cal OSHA within an eight-hour window.

- The subsequent step involves filling out Form 5020, the official record for grave injuries, illnesses, or deaths. This needs to be done within five days of being informed of the incident.

- If a physician seeks information about the employer's workers' compensation insurance carrier, it must be provided promptly.

For employers that are self-insured:

- The report (Form 5020) should be sent directly to the Division of Labor Statistics and Research within five days of learning about the incident.

- When they receive the doctor's report (Form 5021), they have five days to forward it to the Division of Labor Statistics and Research.

In Case of Catastrophes:

For significant or deadly accidents, immediate communication is key. Employers need to inform the nearest Cal OSHA district office by phone or fax within eight hours. This report should detail the affected person's name, employer details, accident specifics, time and date, location, individuals reporting, treatment location for the injured, responding agencies, and a thorough accident description.

Enhancing Construction Safety in California: Obligations and Benefits

The Imperative of Workplace Safety in California

In California, it's a legal necessity for employers to ensure a safe and healthy workspace, especially in the construction sector. Given the risks associated with tasks like excavation, working at elevated heights, using power tools, and managing mobile equipment, employers have an unequivocal duty to shield their workers from potential dangers.

The California Division of Labor Statistics and Research highlights that the construction sector has one of the state's highest work-related injury and fatality rates. Yet, many of these mishaps are preventable when both employers and employees adhere strictly to safety standards. To navigate these requirements efficiently, employers must acquaint themselves with the myriad of local, state, and federal regulations impacting their operations.

Benefits of a Safe and Healthy Work Environment

Safety in the workplace doesn't just shield employees; it is a bulwark for a company's reputation and bottom line. CAL OSHA (California Occupation Safety and Health Act) ensures that working conditions prioritize employee safety. Regularly cited violations touch on areas like scaffolding, excavations, ladders, and more, which should be central themes in safety training initiatives.

Financially, safe workplaces translate to lesser medical costs, diminished product defects, reduced overtime, and fewer expenses related to accommodating injured employees. Such an environment fosters increased productivity, improved morale, and stable labor-management relations, leading to reduced employee turnover. Furthermore, this protective umbrella extends to employees' families, alleviating their stress through income security.

Regulatory Bodies and Their Roles

California boasts several entities dedicated to construction safety and health. Notably:

1. **California Department of Industrial Relations, Division of Occupational Safety and Health (DOSH or CAL OSHA)**: This division not only sets and enforces standards but also offers educational resources for enhanced worker safety.

2. **DOSH Enforcement Unit**: Tasked with upholding regulations, this unit deals with complaints, inspects workplaces, and probes severe job-related injuries or illnesses.

3. **CAL OSHA Consultation Service**: Offers complimentary on-site consultations, aiding employers in resolving safety and health issues.

4. **Occupational Safety and Health Standards Board**: Empowered to modify or introduce new health and safety standards.

5. **Occupational Safety and Health Appeals Board**: Handles appeals relating to orders and penalties from DOSH Enforcement.

Moreover, it's pivotal to remember that the Contractor State License Board can penalize contractors for breaches under other agencies' jurisdiction.

Hiring with Safety in Mind

Emphasizing safety starts even before an employee sets foot on a worksite. It's essential to vet prospective hires thoroughly, ensuring they have a history of adhering to safety protocols. Once onboarded, immediate training regarding potential hazards, safety precautions, and the company's safety code should be mandatory. After all, accidents often stem from unsafe actions more than from unsafe environments.

Best Practices for Ensuring Safety and Health in the Workplace

Introduction to Workplace Safety

For every organization, safeguarding the workplace is a paramount responsibility. At the core of this effort is comprehensive training for all employees, including fresh hires, on established safety practices and the company's Illness and Injury Prevention Program (IIP). The IIP should be detailed, encompassing safe work methodologies and specific guidelines on mitigating job-related hazards.

Understanding Potential Hazards

Jobsites present an array of potential risks. Workers might be exposed to harmful gases, combustible liquids, toxic substances, or dangers like electric shocks and dangerous falls. Depending on tasks, there could be risks from heavy lifting or sustained repetitive motions. Therefore, a robust awareness of construction norms and safety regulations is indispensable.

Medical and Emergency Preparedness

Immediate access to emergency medical services is non-negotiable. It's the employer's duty to ensure there are enough trained personnel to provide first aid when needed. Also, every workplace should be equipped with easily accessible first aid kits.

Regulations and Safety Protocols

Every contractor is mandated to exhibit the "Safety and Health Protection on the Job" poster at all work-centric locations. A written code of safety practices, tailored to the specific work environment, is also a must-have. It's pivotal to recognize that the established safety regulations set the baseline — contractors are always encouraged to go beyond, ensuring even safer work environments.

Personal Protective Equipment (PPE)

Employing the right safety equipment, or PPE, can drastically curtail on-the-job injuries. This encompasses hard hats, protective eyewear, gloves, fall protection devices, face shields, and more, depending on the nature of the job.

Role of the IIP

An effective IIP is central to fostering a secure workspace. CAL OSHA offers consultation services, aiding employers in setting up an impactful IIP and training the workforce on safety and health aspects. The IIP should exude an unequivocal commitment to health and safety, manifested through policies, procedures, incentives, and even disciplinary measures. It's essential to allocate adequate resources for hazard control, equipment procurement, and employee training.

Communication channels should be open, letting employees report hazards, confident that the management will act. Regular audits of workplace conditions and practices ensure consistent safety.

Emergency Action Plans

For organizations with more than ten employees, OSHA mandates a written emergency action plan, displayed prominently. Smaller employers can communicate these plans verbally to their teams.

Employee Rights

It's an employee's prerogative to report any perceived unsafe practices to the Dash enforcement office. Legal provisions protect employees, ensuring they face no retaliation for lodging genuine complaints against unsafe practices.

OSHA Reporting and Workplace Safety Regulations

The Occupational Safety and Health Administration (OSHA) mandates that employers with a workforce of 10 or more employees, excluding those in specified low hazard industries, must maintain three types of records for all work-related illnesses and injuries. These records include OSHA Form 300, Form 300A, and Form 301.

OSHA Form 300 is a log for recording illnesses and injuries at the workplace. It is designed to keep employers, workers, and OSHA informed about the safety conditions of a workplace. For construction operations lasting at least a year, a separate OSHA 300 log must be maintained. This log should include job-related deaths, illnesses (including hearing loss), serious injuries, instances of loss of consciousness, and restrictions of work activity or days away from work.

In addition to the OSHA 300 log, employers must also maintain records of operation and maintenance activities, lockout activities, medical surveillance programs, all trainings, and all inspections.

OSHA Form 300A is a summary of the previous year's work-related injuries and illnesses. It should be publicly posted no later than February 1st and must remain in place until at least April 30th.

OSHA Form 301 is an incident report that provides additional details about each incident recorded in Form 300. If an employee is hospitalized, absent from work for at least one day due to illness or injury, or if a fatality occurs after an occupational incident, the employer is legally required to report the incident to the nearest OSHA office within eight hours. Extensions up to 24 hours may be granted in certain circumstances. If a death occurs within 30 days of the reported incident, the employer must report it within eight hours. However, fatalities occurring after 30 days of a job-related incident are not required to be reported.

To meet the general recording criteria, cases must involve significant illness or injury diagnosed by a physician or other licensed healthcare professional. This is required even if the case does not result in death, days off from work, medical treatment, or loss of consciousness. Additional reports must be made within five days of the incident using Form 5020, the employer's report of occupational injury or illness. In the event of an employee's death resulting from an incident, the employer must file an amended report indicating the death within five days of notification.

If the employer has workers' compensation insurance, a report must be filed with the insurance carrier within five days. If the employer is self-insured, a report must be filed with the Division of Labor Statistics and Research within the same timeframe.

In the event of blasting or other extraordinary accidents, the employer must report to the nearest OSHA office within 24 hours.

Material Safety Data Sheets (MSDS) must be readily available near all workplace chemicals, as per the OSHA Hazard Communication Standard (HCS). These sheets provide precautionary and emergency information about each chemical. Employers whose employees may be exposed to hazardous substances under normal or emergency work conditions are required to provide information and training on the safe handling of these substances and the associated risks.

Before any construction or demolition work begins, a site should be evaluated for hazardous substances. Historical records should be reviewed to identify previous site uses and potential environmental concerns. If hazardous substances are discovered during construction, work must be halted immediately and both the owner and the National Response Center must be notified.

Employers are required to notify all employees exposed to toxic substances or harmful physical agents and inform them of the necessary corrective actions to minimize risk. Employees must be allowed to monitor or measure their exposure to hazards and be granted access to review their own medical and exposure records.

Hazardous Substance Removal and Certification in California

Contractor Certification for Hazardous Removal

For those looking to work in hazardous substance removal, passing a certification examination in this domain is essential. Such a certification becomes imperative when a contractor aims to undertake remedial tasks related to areas designated as hazardous waste sites by the Department of Toxic Substances Control. Additionally, sites mentioned in the national priorities list, as structured by the Comprehensive Environmental Response Compensation and Liability Act of 1980, also demand this certification.

Contractors with existing certifications may need to requalify by passing newer certification exams as stipulated by the Contractors State License Board (CSLB). This is particularly true when there are updates in occupational or public health and safety data. Moreover, employees in this field are expected to align with the Hazardous Waste Operations and Emergency Response (HAZWOPER) standards.

HAZWOPER and OSHA Standards

The HAZWOPER guidelines dictate a detailed work strategy. This involves securing a logistics certification from the Occupational Safety and Health Administration (OSHA) for every employee and supervisor taking part in the hazardous substance removal process. Within this strategy, there's a need for a medical surveillance scheme. A competent individual should be assigned responsibilities like laboratory work scheduling, equipment calibration, evaluation of contaminated material sampling, equipment testing, and test result assessments.

For safeguarding both employees and subcontractors, a site-specific safety and health blueprint is crucial. A conference discussing the intricacies of this plan should precede any actual work. Stakeholders from various groups, including contractors, employers, employees, and their representatives, should be part of this discussion.

Regulations and Notifications in California

In California, employers are bound by the rules defined for ensuring the occupational health and safety of employees, especially those dealing with carcinogenic substances. Operations that utilize regulated carcinogens need to be reported to the Cal/OSHA district office within a two-week window. One such notorious carcinogen is asbestos. Because of its potential health risks, including debilitating and lethal diseases, it's imperative that the Cal/OSHA district office is notified a day before initiating any significant asbestos-related activity.

Should there be a need to dispose of asbestos, notifying entities like the National Emissions Standards for Hazardous Air Pollutants (NESHAP) or the Federal Environmental Protection Agency becomes essential. Strict standards, overseen by the Hazardous Waste Management Branch of the California Department of Toxic Substances Control, are in place for such disposals. Adherence to the Toxic Substances Control Act is non-negotiable.

Lastly, any contractor involved in larger-scale asbestos work, covering an area of 100 square feet or more of asbestos-containing material, should have the necessary Asbestos Certification or AC22 Asbestos Abatement License Classification and must register with the appropriate bodies.

Construction Safety Guidelines: Lead Handling, Power Lines, and OSHA Compliance

Lead-Related Work Protocols

Any supervisor or employee handling lead in their work responsibilities must be certified by the designated authority. Prior to initiating construction, it is obligatory to provide a written pre-job notification about lead work to the nearest authority's district office. Non-compliance can incur heavy fines. The rule applies to every form of lead, from metallic lead to organic lead soaps.

For contractors, the obligation extends to displaying lead work signs, facilitating employee medical check-ups, record-keeping, ensuring employees are privy to monitoring methods, and offering relevant information, training, and certifications. This protocol is especially vital for areas where large surfaces, indoors or outdoors, are covered in lead-based paint.

Buildings constructed before 1978 can be deemed exempt from federal certifications if a certified inspector from the Division of Public Health (DP) ascertains them as lead-free. However, federal penalties loom for contractors bypassing these regulations. Moreover, working on buildings pre-dating 1978 requires contractors to complete an EPA certified renovation course, which holds for five years.

Power Line Safety

Safety around overhead power lines is paramount, and OSHA insists on implementing safety measures such as flags or warning lines to maintain a safe distance. The distance is dictated by the power line's capacity or the equipment in operation. In scenarios where the operator's vision is obscured, hiring a spotter becomes essential.

Acquiring Safety Permits

Before commencing any construction or demolition, acquiring the requisite permits is a must. These permits must be visibly displayed around the job site. Structures surpassing three stories or those that are equivalent to 12 feet per story necessitate permits. Deep excavations, mines, and certain trenches also fall into this category. However, there are exceptions such as emergency repairs and public utility operations.

Regulations, Penalties, and Violations

Authorized officers inspect workplaces in line with OSHA standards. Whenever a violation is identified, the citation needs to be publicly displayed until rectified. Deliberate removal of this citation incurs either hefty fines, jail time, or both. In cases of non-compliance, fines can go up to $7,000 per violation. Persistent violations can attract extra penalties. However, establishments with an IIPP can negotiate these fines based on various factors. If unsatisfied, contractors can challenge these decisions with the OSHA Board within a stipulated timeframe.

Variance from Standards

Contractors can appeal to the Standards Board for variances from specific CAL OSHA standards. For a permanent variance, they must validate that their methods are equally or more protective. Temporary variances are applicable under circumstances like unavailability of resources or recent business acquisitions with existing violations. It is essential, however, that they are actively working towards the safety of their employees and have a plan for full compliance. After appropriate hearings, which employees can attend, these variances might be extended but have a definite limit. Denied variances can be contested with the Standards Board.

Concept Check

1. What must California employers display related to worker rights?
   a) OSHA poster
   b) Cal/OSHA regulations
   c) Labor law notices
   d) Required certifications

2. When must employers notify Cal/OSHA of a workplace fatality?
   a) 24 hours
   b) 48 hours
   c) 1 week
   d) Immediately

3. At what height does fall protection become mandatory?
   a) 4 feet
   b) 5 feet
   c) 6 feet
   d) 10 feet

4. Which area requires guard rails at 7.5 feet high?
   a) Roof openings
   b) Wall holes
   c) Scaffolding
   d) Balconies

5. How much weight should covers withstand?
   a) Worker weight
   b) Double the load
   c) Max vehicle weight
   d) Tripled load

6. How often should warning lines be marked?
   a) Every 3 feet
   b) Every 6 feet
   c) Every 10 feet
   d) No requirements

7. What is a Personal Fall Arrest System designed to do?
   a) Secure tools
   b) Arrest falls
   c) Anchor equipment
   d) Connect workers

8. How far can a worker potentially fall with PFAS?
    a) 3 feet
    b) 5 feet
    c) 6 feet
    d) 10 feet

9. When are safety nets required for fall protection?
    a) 10+ feet falls
    b) 15+ feet falls
    c) 25+ feet falls
    d) 30+ feet falls

10. When is a permit required for scaffolding?
    a) Over 2 stories tall
    b) Over 3 stories tall
    c) Over 4 stories tall
    d) Over 5 stories tall

11. How much weight must scaffolds support beyond their own?
    a) Double the load
    b) Triple the load
    c) Quadruple the load
    d) No requirement

12. When are railings mandatory on work platforms?
    a) Over 4 feet high
    b) Over 6 feet high
    c) Over 7.5 feet high
    d) Over 10 feet high

13. What is the minimum plank thickness for scaffolds?
    a) 1 inch
    b) 1.5 inches
    c) 2 inches
    d) 3 inches

14. When is retraining mandatory for scaffold workers?
    a) Annually
    b) After an accident
    c) If proficiency is lacking
    d) After assembly

15. When should ladders NOT be used?
    a) High winds
    b) Poor visibility
    c) User is medicated
    d) All of the above

16. How many contact points should be maintained on a ladder?
    a) One
    b) Two
    c) Three
    d) Four

17. When are fiberglass ladders preferable?
    a) Outdoors
    b) Heavy loads
    c) Around electricity
    d) Wet areas

18. What should NOT be used as a standing surface on step ladders?
    a) Top cap
    b) Pail shelf
    c) Top step
    d) All of the above

19. What is required for a 32-foot two-section extension ladder?
    a) 48-inch overlap
    b) 36-inch overlap
    c) 62-inch overlap
    d) No overlap needed

20. What injury can result in paralysis or death?
    a) Electrical shock
    b) Electrocution
    c) Thermal burns
    d) Indirect injuries

21. What are arc or flash burns caused by?
    a) Electric current passage
    b) Heat from equipment
    c) Electrical explosions
    d) Circuit overloads

22. What helps identify potential electrical hazards?
    a) GFCIs
    b) Warning signs
    c) Routine inspections
    d) Circuit diagrams

23. What can indicate an electrical issue?
    a) Burning smells
    b) Warm equipment
    c) Tripped breakers
    d) All of the above

24. What's risky when handling electrical tools?
    a) Lifting by cords
    b) High voltage use
    c) Improper grounding
    d) Lack of training

25. What must PPE used by workers comply with?
    a) Company policy
    b) ANSI standards
    c) OSHA regulations
    d) Manufacturer instructions

26. Which PPE offers electrical protection up to 20,000 volts?
    a) Class A hard hats
    b) Class B hard hats
    c) Class C hard hats
    d) Face shields

27. What warrants a workplace hearing conservation program?
    a) 80 dB noise exposure
    b) 85 dB noise exposure
    c) 90 dB noise exposure
    d) 95 dB noise exposure

28. Which material is prohibited in protective gloves?
    a) Leather
    b) Cotton
    c) Asbestos
    d) Rubber

29. What should footwear protect against in certain jobs?
    a) Slippage
    b) Impacts
    c) Electrical shocks
    d) All of the above

30. What does the NFPA use to classify fires?
    a) Temperature
    b) Size
    c) Fuel source
    d) Cause

31. What extinguisher is suited for electrical fires?
    a) Water (APW)
    b) Carbon dioxide (CO_2)
    c) Dry chemical
    d) Wet chemical

32. What is the primary extinguisher for cooking oil fires?
    a) Water (APW)
    b) Carbon dioxide (CO_2)
    c) Dry chemical
    d) Wet chemical

33. Where should you position yourself when using an extinguisher?
    a) Upwind
    b) Near an exit
    c) Near the fire
    d) Downwind

34. How should you direct the extinguisher nozzle?
    a) At the smoke
    b) At the base
    c) At the flames
    d) At the perimeter

35. What size fire should an extinguisher be used on?
    a) Large spreading fire
    b) Medium contained fire
    c) Small manageable fire
    d) Any size fire

36. What provides guidance on creating an IIPP?
    a) Federal OSHA
    b) State OSHA
    c) Labor unions
    d) Insurance agencies

37. What demonstrates management's safety commitment?
    a) Documented practices
    b) Regular inspections
    c) Anonymous reporting
    d) Hiring competent staff

38. What should occur after safety incidents?
    a) Training refreshers
    b) Policy updates
    c) Thorough investigations
    d) Increased documentation

39. What should be provided with required safety gear?
    a) Proper training
    b) Cleaning services
    c) Replacement schedule
    d) Optional usage

40. When should updated training occur?
    a) Annually
    b) Periodically
    c) With new equipment
    d) With new processes

41. What must medical provisions include?
    a) Health insurance
    b) On-site first aid
    c) Doctor's contact information
    d) Ambulance services

42. What must be done before any excavation in California?
    a) Survey for utilities
    b) Notify Underground Service Alert
    c) Obtain digging permits
    d) Develop safety plan

43. How many days before digging should USA be notified?
    a) Same day
    b) 1-2 days
    c) 3-5 days
    d) 10-14 days

44. How far should spoil piles be from the trench edge?
    a) 1 foot
    b) 2 feet
    c) 3 feet
    d) 5 feet

45. Who must oversee design for deep trenches?
    a) Competent person
    b) Safety manager
    c) Licensed engineer
    d) Equipment operator

46. What is the sloping ratio for Type B soil?
    a) 0.5:1
    b) 1:1
    c) 1.5:1
    d) 2:1

47. What helps prevent trench wall collapse?
    a) Spoil pile distance
    b) Shoring and benching
    c) Gradual sloping
    d) Soil moisture monitoring

48. Which form records work-related injuries and illnesses?
    a) Form 100
    b) Form 200
    c) Form 300
    d) Form 400

49. Where must the annual data summary be displayed?
    a) Company website
    b) Main entrance
    c) All work areas
    d) HR department

50. What is the deadline for fatality reporting to Cal/OSHA?
    a) 24 hours
    b) 48 hours
    c) 1 week
    d) 8 hours

51. How long does an employer have to file Form 5020?
    a) 24 hours
    b) 48 hours
    c) 5 days
    d) 1 week

52. What must be provided to physicians upon request?
    a) Form 5021
    b) Insurance details
    c) Log 300
    d) Employee contact info

53. Where do self-insured employers send Form 5020?
    a) Nearest Cal/OSHA office
    b) State Labor Department
    c) Division of Labor Statistics
    d) Workers' compensation board

54. How can a safe workplace impact medical costs?
    a) Increase them
    b) Reduce them
    c) Eliminate them
    d) Double them

55. What does the DOSH Enforcement Unit handle?
    a) Standards
    b) Inspections
    c) Consultations
    d) Appeals

56. What impacts contractor penalties besides CAL OSHA?
    a) Labor unions
    b) Trade associations
    c) CSLB
    d) Insurance agencies

57. What helps ensure prospective hires value safety?
    a) Reference checks
    b) Safety exams
    c) Trial periods
    d) Drug tests

58. When is PPE necessary?
    a) During meetings
    b) Only when required
    c) For all tasks
    d) Only for managers

59. Who should review emergency action plans?
    a) Government agencies
    b) Employees
    c) Insurance providers
    d) Safety consultants

60. What protects employees who report safety issues?
    a) Whistleblower laws
    b) Union membership
    c) IIP policies
    d) Industry groups

61. How often must a separate OSHA 300 log be maintained for construction sites?
    a) Quarterly
    b) Monthly
    c) Annually
    d) Weekly

62. What requires reporting an incident to OSHA within 8 hours?
    a) Property damage
    b) Minor injury
    c) Hospitalization
    d) Near miss

63. When must blasting accidents be reported?
    a) 8 hours
    b) 24 hours
    c) 48 hours
    d) 1 week

64. What must supervisors have per HAZWOPER?
    a) Lab experience
    b) Medical training
    c) OSHA certification
    d) Engineering degree

65. When must Cal/OSHA be notified before asbestos work?
    a) 1 week
    b) 2 days
    c) 1 month
    d) 1 day

66. Who must be certified for lead work?
    a) Contractors
    b) Supervisors
    c) Employees
    d) All of the above

67. What incurs fines for lead work violations?
    a) Lack of training
    b) No spotters
    c) Missing signs
    d) Not notifying officials

68. When can pre-1978 buildings skip lead inspections?
    a) If recently painted
    b) If owner certifies no lead
    c) If inspector deems lead-free
    d) If less than 3 stories

69. What helps maintain distance from power lines?
    a) Warning signs
    b) Safety cones
    c) Guardrails
    d) Warning lines

70. What is the limit for temporary variances?
    a) 1 year
    b) 18 months
    c) 2 years
    d) No limit

Concept Check Solutions

1. A) OSHA poster. Employers in California must display the official OSHA poster outlining workers' occupational safety rights and responsibilities where employees can easily view it. Cal/OSHA regulations, labor law notices, and certifications are not mandatory postings.

2. D) Immediately. Employers in California must notify Cal/OSHA immediately about any work-related fatality. Waiting 24-48 hours or up to 1 week does not meet the urgent reporting requirement for work-related deaths.

3. C) 6 feet. OSHA mandates fall protection anytime there is a risk of workers falling 6 feet or more to a lower level from unprotected sides, edges, holes, roofs, excavations etc. Lower heights of 4-5 feet or 10+ feet do not trigger the fall protection requirement.

4. D) Balconies. Guard rails are required by OSHA at elevated work areas 7.5 feet or higher above lower levels, including balconies, porches, and platforms. Roof openings, wall holes, and scaffolding have different fall protection requirements.

5. B) Double the load. OSHA states covers and hole barricades must withstand double the weight of workers, equipment, and materials expected. Worker weight, max vehicle weight, or triple loads are incorrect.

6. B) Every 6 feet. Warning lines used for roofing work zones as fall protection must be clearly marked every 6 feet as per OSHA regulations. 3, 10, or no required markings do not comply.

7. B) Arrest falls. Personal Fall Arrest Systems (PFAS) are designed specifically to arrest and stop a worker's fall midway down when working at heights to prevent impact injuries. Securing tools, anchoring equipment, and connecting workers are not the purpose of PFAS.

8. C) 6 feet. Properly designed PFAS must restrict a worker's potential fall to a maximum of 6 feet to prevent contact with lower surfaces when arresting the fall. Shorter 3-5 feet or longer 10+ feet falls exceed PFAS equipment capacities.

9. C) 25+ feet falls. Safety nets become required for fall protection when working 25+ feet above ground/water where ladders, scaffolds, or other conventional measures are not feasible. Lower height thresholds of 10, 15, or 30+ feet do not mandate nets.

10. B) Over 3 stories tall. In the United States, scaffolding exceeding 3 stories or 36 feet in height requires a permit per OSHA regulations before construction. Lower 2-story or higher 4-5 story thresholds do not mandate permits.

11. C) Quadruple the load. Scaffolds must have a safety factor allowing them to support their own weight plus 4 times the intended working load per OSHA. Double or triple load capacities are inadequate while no specific requirement does not comply.

12. C) Over 7.5 feet high. OSHA mandates that manufacturer-provided railings be installed on scaffold work platforms elevated 7.5 feet or higher to protect from falls. Lower 4-6 feet heights or higher 10+ feet do not define the railing requirement.

13. C) 2 inches. Scaffold planking must meet OSHA's minimum thickness standard of 2 inches for safety. Insufficient 1-1.5 inch planks or overbuilt 3+ inch planks do not meet requirements.

14. C) If proficiency is lacking. Retraining is compulsory for scaffold workers if their proficiency seems deficient, not routinely annual, post-accident, or post-assembly. Assessing proficiency determines retraining need.

15. D) All of the above. Ladders should not be utilized if the user is medicated, in poor health, or facing hazardous conditions like high winds or poor visibility that can compromise stability and footing. Each scenario makes ladder use potentially unsafe.

16. C) Three. When climbing any ladder, maintaining three points of contact is vital - two hands and one foot stable on the ladder at all times. This provides optimal stability and safety. Fewer contact points create risk.

17. C) Around electricity. On construction sites, fiberglass ladders are preferable when working around electrical sources since fiberglass is non-conductive for added safety. Outdoors, heavy loads, and wet areas do not dictate fiberglass specificity.

18. D) All of the above. Step ladder top caps, pail shelves, and top steps should never be utilized as standing support surfaces per OSHA. Each part poses serious fall risks.

19. B) 36-inch overlap. On two-section extension ladders up to 32 feet, OSHA mandates a minimum 36-inch overlap of the two sections for safety and stability. 48 or 62-inch overlaps are excessive, while no overlap fails to meet the overlap requirement.

20. B) Electrocution. Electrocution, which involves a lethal electrical shock, can lead to severe burns, nerve damage, cardiac arrest, paralysis, and potentially death. Electrical shock, burns, and indirect injuries are not usually fatal.

21. C) Electrical explosions. Arc or flash burns result from intense heat caused by an electric current explosion or arc as it jumps from one conductor to another. Electric current passage, equipment heat, and circuit overloads do not cause arc/flash burns.

22. C) Routine inspections. Potential electrical hazards are best recognized through regular, thorough safety inspections checking for exposed wires, damaged equipment, overloads, improper grounding, smell/heat indicators, etc. GFCIs, signs, and diagrams cannot identify hazards.

23. D) All of the above. Tripped breakers, burning smells from overheating, and unusually warm equipment can all signify electrical issues like faults, damage, or overloads. Each observation flags potentially hazardous conditions.

24. A) Lifting by cords. Most risky when handling electrical tools is lifting or carrying them by the cord, which can cause tears and expose live wires leading to shocks or electrocution. High voltage use, grounding, and training do not directly heighten injury risk.

25. B) ANSI standards. Personal protective equipment used by workers must comply with applicable ANSI standards for the specific type of PPE. Company policies, OSHA regulations, and manufacturer instructions do not set definitive PPE standards.

26. B) Class B hard hats. Of the ANSI hard hat classes, only Class B head protection offers maximal electrical shock protection, guarding up to 20,000 volts. Class A reaches 2200 volts, while Class C has no electrical rating. Face shields are not ANSI classified.

27. B) 85 dB noise exposure. A continuous 8-hour exposure of 85 decibels warrants a workplace hearing conservation program as per OSHA. Lower 80 dB or higher 90-95 dB averages do not automatically necessitate conservation programs.

28. C) Asbestos. Asbestos fibers in gloves are explicitly prohibited by OSHA because asbestos poses long-term health hazards like mesothelioma when inhaled. Leather, cotton, rubber containments are not banned.

29. D) All of the above. OSHA requires footwear to guard against slips, impacts, electrical shocks, and other risks based on workplace hazards present. Protection against a single hazard does not suffice.

30. C) Fuel source. The National Fire Protection Agency (NFPA) categorizes fires into classes based on the type of fuel feeding the fire - ordinary combustibles, flammable liquids/gases, electrical equipment, etc. Temperature, size, and cause do not dictate NFPA class divisions.

31. B) Carbon dioxide (CO2). For electrical equipment fires, a carbon dioxide (CO2) extinguisher is ideally suited and approved. Water, dry chemical, and wet chemical extinguishers are not applicable for Class C electrical fires.

32. D) Wet chemical. Wet chemical extinguishers are specially designed by NFPA standards to extinguish cooking oil or kitchen-based Class K fires. Water, CO2, and dry chemical are not effective on K fires.

33. B) Near an exit. When tackling a fire with an extinguisher, always position yourself near an exit for a quick escape if the fire grows beyond the extinguisher's capacity. Upwind, near the fire itself, or downwind positions risk entrapment.

34. B) At the base. Following the "A" of PASS, the extinguisher nozzle should be aimed at the base of the fire where fuel meets air. Targeting smoke, flames, or perimeter is less effective.

35. C) Small manageable fire. Extinguishers are only intended, designed, and capable of extinguishing small, manageable fires in the initial stages. Large spreading fires require professional firefighter response.

36. B) State OSHA. California's state OSHA agency, Cal/OSHA, provides guidance and free consultation services to employers to assist them in developing an effective, compliant Injury and Illness Prevention Program. Federal OSHA, unions, and insurance agencies do not play this role.

37. A) Documented practices. Per Cal/OSHA, management demonstrates its commitment to safety through robust organizational policies, accountability structures, and measures documented in writing as part of the IIPP. Inspections, reporting, and hiring alone do not exhibit commitment.

38. C) Thorough investigations. Following safety incidents, the IIPP mandates comprehensive investigations by competent staff to determine causal factors and prevent future occurrences through improvements. Training, policies, documentation are secondary actions.

39. A) Proper training. The IIPP stipulates that when the employer mandates certain safety gear use, they must provide the gear AND training on its proper use to maximize efficacy. Cleaning services, replacement schedules, and optional usage undermine safety mandates.

40. C) With new equipment. The IIPP obligates additional or updated worker training whenever new equipment, tools, machinery or production processes are introduced to ensure safe operation in the changed environment. New training is not mandated annually, periodically, or just for processes.

41. B) On-site first aid. To prepare for emergencies, employers must maintain trained first aid providers on-site and ensure first aid kits are accessible, per Cal/OSHA IIPP standards. Insurance, doctor contacts, and ambulances are beneficial but not mandated.

42. B) Notify Underground Service Alert. According to California law, excavators must notify Underground Service Alert (USA) prior to any digging or excavation to get underground utilities marked. Surveying, permits, and planning do not fulfill the USA notification mandate.

43. D) 10-14 days. Excavators must contact USA at minimum 2 days but no more than 14 calendar days before starting digging. Same day, 1-2 days, and 3-5 days fail to satisfy the 2-14 day advance USA notification window.

44. B) 2 feet. OSHA requires spoil piles from trench digging be kept at least 2 feet back from the edge to prevent hazardous collapses. 1 foot is insufficient and 3-5 feet may be excessive depending on the project.

45. C) Licensed engineer. For trenches exceeding 20 feet depth, a professional licensed engineer must oversee the shoring system design for safety. Competent persons, managers, and operators lack engineering credentials.

46. B) 1:1. OSHA standards mandate a maximum soil slope ratio of 1:1 for Type B soils like silt and clay that are prone to shifting and collapse. 0.5:1, 1.5:1, and 2:1 exceed Type B limits.

47. B) Shoring and benching. Installing shoring frameworks and benching or stepping the trench sides are the most direct methods for preventing hazardous collapses. Sloping, spoils, and monitoring do not actively reinforce.

48. C) Form 300. California employers must use Form 300 to document all work-related injuries and illnesses that meet certain severity criteria, such as medical treatment beyond first aid. Form 100, Form 200, and Form 400 are not used for this mandatory recordkeeping.

49. B) Main entrance. A summary of the 300 Log data must be publicly displayed at the workplace's main entrance from February 1st to April 30th each year for establishments with 11+ employees. Websites, work areas, and HR departments are not compliant display locations.

50. D) 8 hours. Employers have a maximum of 8 hours to notify the nearest Cal/OSHA office by phone or fax in the event of any work-related fatality, as per urgent reporting regulations. 24 hours, 48 hours, and 1 week exceed the 8-hour limit.

51. C) 5 days. For serious injuries, illnesses or fatalities, employers have 5 calendar days to fill out and submit the required Form 5020 report to Cal/OSHA after learning of the incident. 24 hours, 48 hours, and 1 week do not meet the 5-day deadline.

52. B) Insurance details. If requested, employers must promptly provide physicians caring for injured workers with details of their workers' compensation insurance carrier. Form 5021, Logs, and contact info are not mandated disclosures.

53. C) Division of Labor Statistics. For self-insured employers, Form 5020 must be sent directly to the Division of Labor Statistics and Research within 5 days of learning of a catastrophic incident, not Cal/OSHA, the Labor Department, or the workers' compensation board.

54. B) Reduce them. A safe, healthy work environment can lead to reduced medical costs for employers by preventing injuries that necessitate treatment. Safety precautions do not increase, eliminate, or double medical costs.

55. B) Inspections. The DOSH Enforcement Unit specifically handles inspections, complaints, and investigations to enforce CAL OSHA workplace safety regulations. Standards, consultations, and appeals are handled by other divisions.

56. C) CSLB. The Contractor State License Board can levy penalties against licensed contractors for safety violations under other agencies like CAL OSHA. Unions, trade groups, and insurers do not penalize contractor licenses.

57. A) Reference checks. Thoroughly checking a prospective hire's references can provide insights into their safety records and commitment to following protocols at past jobs. Exams, trials, and drug tests are secondary screening tools.

58. B) Only when required. Personal protective equipment is necessary when specific tasks or environments present hazards that PPE can mitigate. Routine meetings, all tasks, and manager roles rarely necessitate PPE unless a risk assessment indicates the need.

59. B) Employees. Emergency action plans must be reviewed by all employees to ensure familiarity with the proper emergency response and evacuation procedures. Government, insurers, consultants play no direct role.

60. A) Whistleblower laws. Whistleblower provisions protect employees from retaliation when reporting safety issues in good faith. Union membership, IIPP policies, and industry groups do not explicitly prevent retaliation.

61. C) Annually. For construction projects lasting at least one year, employers must maintain a separate OSHA 300 log specifically for that site on an annual basis. Quarterly, monthly, and weekly logs are not mandated.

62. C) Hospitalization. If an employee is hospitalized due to a work-related incident, the employer must report it to OSHA within 8 hours. Property damage, minor injuries, and near misses do not trigger this urgent reporting requirement.

63. B) 24 hours. Extraordinary accidents like blasting must be reported to the closest OSHA office within 24 hours of occurring. 8 hours, 48 hours, and 1 week do not meet the urgent 24-hour reporting criteria.

64. C) OSHA certification. Under HAZWOPER, supervisors partaking in hazardous substance removal must secure logistics certification from OSHA. Lab experience, medical training, and engineering degrees do not fulfill this mandatory requirement.

65. D) 1 day. For significant asbestos jobs, Cal/OSHA must be informed at least 1 day prior to work initiation to allow hazard review. 1 week, 2 days, and 1 month are not compliant with the 24 hour asbestos notification requirement.

66. D) All of the above. Per regulations, any supervisor, contractor, or employee handling lead materials in their work must be certified by the designated authority to do lead-related construction or abatement.

67. D) Not notifying officials. Failure to provide proper pre-job notification about lead work to local officials can result in substantial fines for violations. Lack of training, spotters, or signs incur smaller penalties.

68. C) If inspector deems lead-free. Pre-1978 buildings can skip federal lead inspection/abatement requirements if a certified Division of Public Health inspector affirms the building as lead-free. Self-certification, recent paint, and size do not waive the need for qualified lead-free determination.

69. D) Warning lines. OSHA mandates erecting warning lines at the appropriate distance from power lines to maintain safe clearance during equipment operation. Signs, cones, and guardrails are less definitive methods.

70. C) 2 years. Temporary CAL OSHA standard variances have a definite limit of 2 years. Permanent variances have no expiration, while 1 year and 18 months fall short of the temporary variance duration cap.

General Building (B)

Preparing a Construction Site: From Clearing to Grading in California

Site Preparation Basics

Before kicking off a major construction project, it's imperative to ready the site. The initial steps include lot clearing, which doesn't only mean removing vehicles and large debris but also ensuring curbs and gutters are unobstructed. Proper drainage is vital during construction; a clear system prevents blockages and stops pollutants from the site from reaching public water systems.

Underground Service Alert in California

One indispensable resource in California is the Underground Service Alert. Offered free of charge, it's a damage prevention service that assesses excavation plans. Before any digging starts, they send a crew to the location to provide critical information about the site, including potential issues and the positioning of underground utilities. California mandates contacting this service between two to 14 days prior to beginning excavation. Ignoring this can lead to hefty fines, reaching up to $50,000 if done intentionally.

This service employs a combination of color-coded and abbreviated markers to denote each utility. For example, yellow indicates gas, oil, or steam, blue is used for potable water, and orange marks communication or alarm lines. Additionally, symbols such as "W" for water or "SL" for street lighting are used.

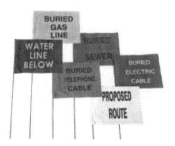

Leveling and Understanding Soil Types

After clearing the lot and marking utilities, the land needs leveling. This involves excavation, filling gaps, and compacting the added soil to a minimum of 90% as per the state's building code, ensuring no subsequent soil settling that might jeopardize the foundation.

Soils have a pivotal role in this process, primarily divided into granular and cohesive types. While granular soil consists of larger particles like sand, making it less stable, cohesive soil is sticky and compact due to its clay content.

These soils are further classified as:

- Type A: Highly cohesive and the most stable.

- Type B: A blend of granular and cohesive properties, with moderate stability.

- Type C: Predominantly granular and the least stable.

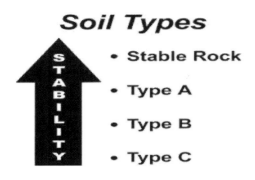
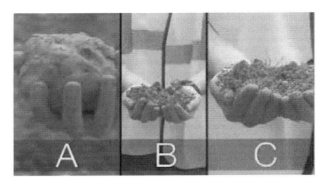

Staking and Grading the Property

To guide the leveling process, survey stakes are used. These are visibly placed, marked either with an 'F' (indicating material addition) or 'C' (indicating material removal). They further detail the volume of material needed and the desired grade level.

Grading ensures a flat or sloped surface within the construction zone. While structures often need a flat base, slopes are essential for drainage. Utilizing a single reference point and a transit, stakes are elevated to match the original transit level, ensuring a smooth, level area, primed for laying the foundation.

Concrete

Concrete Formwork

Concrete formwork is the process of creating molds that shape the concrete as it is poured. This is the first task undertaken by a construction crew when starting a project. After the trenches are dug, outlining the building, forms are set inside them to create a structured concrete pour, which will then provide the building's outline. The initial forms are set in place to create an outline for the entire building, including the forms for the columns that will provide structural support. Some forms may be removed to complete any necessary formwork. Inside the building outline, the forms are set using form boards and rebar stakes for stability. For safety, orange safety caps should be placed on any protruding rebar. The concrete is poured inside the forms, which are then removed after the concrete has dried.

Footing Formwork

Once the footings are excavated and cleared, forms are placed in them. These forms allow the crew to shape the footing, ensuring that they meet the size requirements set by the state of California. Form boards are used to size out the footings and columns. There are two types of formwork classes: Class one formwork is used for temporary or light loads, while Class two formwork is used for structures that will encounter heavy loads.

Class 1 Formwork

Class 2 Formwork

Footings

Footings are used to prevent the foundation from settling and provide structural support. They are necessary for building multi-story structures. Footings help prevent issues that can occur due to soil shifting or settling over time. They are made with concrete and rebar and are poured into the previously excavated trenches. The size of the footing depends on the weight that the column must support. The taller the building, the larger the footing needs to be. The state of California has specific size requirements for footings based on the building's height.

Footing Excavation

Once the building's layout is marked, the excavation for the footings can begin. The footing should extend at least 12 inches below the soil for a one-story building in undisturbed soil, and below the frost line to prevent freezing water from cracking them. The required size of footings would increase if intended to support 2 to 3 story buildings or if the soil has a lower load-bearing value. Compaction is typically required. Compaction is a process of increasing soil density and removing air, usually by mechanical means. The size of the individual soil particles does not change, neither is water removed. Purposeful compaction is intended to improve the strength and stiffness of soil. A soil test is used to determine the load-bearing value of the soil. The excavation is finished by hand for precision. There may also be smaller interior footings needed, which are generally dug out by hand.

Rebar

Rebar is used to reinforce and increase the tensile strength and ductility of the concrete. Without rebar, a concrete foundation and structural support would be highly prone to cracking. It also increases the concrete's ability to withstand forces that pull concrete apart. Deformed bars are made with carbon steel and have ridges on their exterior for better anchoring. They have a high strength-to-weight ratio and can be welded together easily. They can also be easily bent and manipulated as needed.

Reinforcing Main Fields

The spacing of the rebar varies based on the area it is being used in. In the main fields where the floors will typically be poured, the rebar should be spaced in an 18-inch by 18-inch grid across the ground. The grid should be tighter at 15 inches by 18 inches around the sides. The overlapping points of the perpendicular rebar should be tied together by wire ties to prevent the rebar from slipping before the concrete hardens. Once the grid is properly laid out, it will be elevated using chairs. This allows the rebar to become engulfed within the middle of the concrete as it is poured over the top of the grid.

Reinforcing Stem Walls

Concrete stem walls surround the outline of a building. When reinforced with one-half inch diameter rebar, the rebar itself should be placed three inches from the top of the footing as well as three inches from the bottom of a footing. The rebar should be spaced out in a similar fashion as outlined in the main fields, no more than 18 inches apart. If the rebar is spaced greater than 18 inches apart, additional rebar must be used to lessen the gap.

The Building Code stipulates that the standard overlap for rebar should be 30 times its diameter. For example, a three-quarter inch diameter rebar, also known as number six rebar, should have an overlap of 22.5 inches. Similarly, a number five rebar or five-eighths inch rebar should have an overlap of 18.75 inches.

In the context of concrete stem walls designed under the California Residential Code (CRC), there should be a minimum of one number four bar positioned within 12 inches from the top of the wall and another one located 3 to 4 inches from the bottom of the footing.

Concrete slabs should have a thickness of 3.5 inches or more. If the slab is intended for use as a living area floor or garage, it should be reinforced with a rebar grid or wire mesh. A waterproof layer should be placed beneath the slab to separate it from the soil and living areas. The footings for the concrete slabs should have 21 half-inch thick rears or walls that will support weight in garage door openings.

The concrete section contains a diagram labeled "Concrete Slab Construction" that illustrates the components of slab construction. This diagram shows the spacing of anchor bolts, such as the 5/8 inch anchor bolts required for seismic design category E. These should be spaced at 6 feet on center for a one-story building or 4 feet on center for a two-story building. They should also be placed a minimum of four inches and a maximum of 12 inches from the edge of the sill plate.

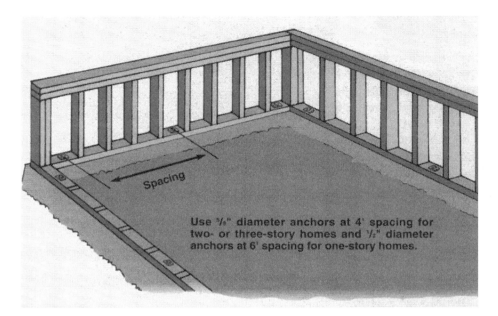

Use ⅜" diameter anchors at 4' spacing for two- or three-story homes and ½" diameter anchors at 6' spacing for one-story homes.

For proper grounding, an electrode within the concrete foundation must meet certain criteria. It must be encased by at least two inches of concrete, be at or near the bottom of the footing or foundation, and the concrete must be in contact with the ground. The electrode should consist of at least 20 feet of rebar that is at least half an inch thick or 20 feet of solid copper as a conductor.

When the site is prepared, the concrete can be poured. The concrete will be delivered by a concrete truck and can be poured directly onto the site or delivered by a concrete boom truck for more precision and flexibility. After pouring, a concrete vibrator is used to eliminate any potential air pockets that could weaken the concrete. The concrete is then leveled and smoothed by the crew to ensure a flat, smooth finish as it dries.

There are several types of concrete mixtures, each with varying ratios of water, sand, and rock, and each ideal for different purposes. The four main types of concrete mixture ratios are rich, standard, medium, and lean.

Rich concrete mixtures contain one part cement, two parts sand or fine aggregate, and three parts coarse aggregate. This type of mixture is used for concrete roads and waterproof structures. Standard mixtures are used for reinforced work floors, roofs, columns, arches, tanks, sewers, conduits, and so on. Medium mixtures are used for foundations, walls, abutments, piers, and so forth. Lean mixtures, which contain one part cement, three parts sand or fine aggregate, and six parts coarse aggregate, are used for all mass concrete work, large foundations, backing for stone masonry, and so on.

There are five types of Portland cement used for different construction purposes. Type one is normal and used for most general purposes. Type two is moderate and used when precautions against moderate sulfate attack are important. Type three is high early strength and used when high early strength is needed. Type four is low heat of hydration and used when hydration heat must be minimized in large volume applications. Type five is high sulfate resistance and used as a precaution against severe sulfate action.

The time it takes for concrete to dry depends on several factors, including the water to cement ratio, the size of the particles within the cement mixture, the chemical makeup of the mixture, the ambient temperature and weather conditions, the temperature of the concrete being placed and if any admixtures have been added to the concrete. The most significant factor is the volume and, more specifically, the depth of the pour.

There are two set times in construction: the initial set time, when the concrete hardens significantly but cannot yet reliably support weight, and the final set time, when the concrete hardens to the point where it can withstand a significant amount of weight.

The concrete process involves preparing the site, pouring the concrete, leveling and smoothing it out, and removing chairs and forms. The minimum strength of the concrete for foundation construction should reach at least 3000 pounds per square inch when fully dry. After 28 days, the cement is smoothed out, a process that must be done with the proper equipment and timing.

The stages of concrete setting include the initial 2 to 4 hours when the concrete has begun to set but cannot support any weight, and 24 hours when the concrete should be able to support someone standing on it. However, it is still prone to smudges and indenting if a moderate amount of weight is applied.

The process of concrete curing and finishing involves several stages, each with its own specific requirements and timeframes.

Firstly, the concrete needs to be allowed to cure. After being poured, the concrete should not be subjected to heavy weight or foot traffic. After three days, the concrete should be able to withstand normal foot traffic, but not heavy loads. After seven days, the concrete should be able to support heavier loads and is nearing its maximum load-bearing capacity. However, heavy machinery should still be avoided. After 28 days, the concrete has fully hardened and can support up to its maximum capacity, allowing for the use of heavy machinery.

The finishing process of concrete involves several steps. The first is bleeding, which involves removing any liquid water that rises to the surface of the mixture after it has been poured. This water should be allowed to evaporate naturally, as troweling it back into the concrete can dilute the mixture and weaken its strength.

Next is screeding, which is the process of smoothing the concrete after it has been poured. This is typically done using a screed, a long flat board or beam made of wood or aluminum.

Leveling is then done to ensure that the surface of the concrete will dry flat and even. This is typically done using a screed.

Jointing is the process of placing planned cuts into the concrete to prevent it from cracking as it expands and contracts due to temperature changes. Joints should be placed 2 to 3 feet apart per inch of thickness on the concrete slab. The depth of the joint should be 25% of the thickness of the slab.

There are three types of joints: control joints, isolation joints, and construction joints. Control joints are common on sidewalks, isolation joints are used to separate the concrete slab from other materials, and construction joints are used for large projects where the entire slab cannot be poured at once.

Control joints (I.e. contraction joints)	Isolation Joints (I.e. expansion Joints)	Construction joint or pour joint

Floating is the process of using a tool to give the surface of the concrete a smooth finish. This is followed by troweling, which is similar to floating but uses a tool with a harder flat edge to give the concrete a strong and dense surface.

The final stage of finishing concrete is broom finishing, which involves dragging a broom across the surface of the cement to create small grooves for traction.

A slump test is used to measure the consistency of the concrete. This test involves filling a metal mold in the shape of a traffic cone with concrete in three stages, then removing the cone and measuring how much the mixture has slumped. The results of this test can indicate whether the concrete slump is consistent across different batches.

Concrete Slump Cone Test

Concrete Air Meter Test

Framing and Structural Components

This section discusses the foundational aspects of framing and structural components, accounting for nearly 25% of the general building exam's content. While our emphasis is primarily on light wood framing and construction nails, readers should note that metal framing is less frequently covered in the examination.

Understanding Construction Nails

Among the most basic yet versatile tools in construction are nails. Used primarily for joining wood pieces, they come in diverse shapes, sizes, and metals. Though steel is a popular choice, other materials like aluminum, brass, and stainless steel are also employed, with the latter being particularly favorable in corrosive environments. To bolster their efficiency and resist rust, these nails might have coatings such as galvanization, glue, or cement.

When referencing nail sizes, the term 'penny size' is used. This spans from two penny (2D), which measures an inch, to 60 penny (60D) nails that extend to six inches. Nails less than an inch are termed 'brads', whereas those exceeding six inches are 'spikes'. It's vital to select an appropriate length, as ideally, two-thirds of the nail should embed into the primary material.

There's a wide range of nail types, each tailored for specific tasks. This includes common nails, box nails, drywall nails, and more, each catering from heavy-duty construction to lighter tasks.

Framing Basics

In the realm of wall framing, the bottom plate, often called the sole or sill plate, is the base for the studs. When this plate is positioned atop the foundation, it's branded a sill plate, necessitating anchorage to the foundation with bolts. A contemporary practice employs a polyethylene-based product, dubbed the 'sill sealer', to thwart air leaks and moisture transmission from concrete to wood.

Studs, which form the core of the framing structure, should be placed with their broader dimension jutting out. Typically, residential structures employ two by four-inch studs. The spacing depends on their load; 24 inches apart for a roof or ceiling support, while a two-story structure demands a 16-inch spacing.

Key structural features to note include the requirement of a double top plate for all bearing and exterior walls, and the presence of headers above doors and windows, ensuring robust support. Moreover, any wall that extends up to a ceiling or floor must incorporate fire blocking.

FIRE BLOCKING - SOFFIT

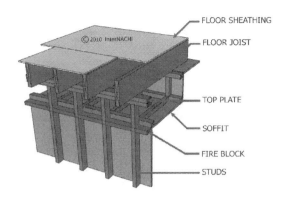

Building Codes and Standards

To meet safety and habitability standards, various stipulations have been established. These include a minimum ceiling height of 7 feet for most habitable spaces, and room size requirements to ensure comfort and functionality, such as a 120 square-foot room in dwellings and a 70 square-foot criterion for other rooms, barring kitchens.

The Art of Using Nails in Construction

When working with nails or approved fasteners in wall sheathing, it's imperative to drive them flush against a structural wood panel, ensuring you don't fracture the wood by hammering too aggressively. For the CSLB contractors license exam, comprehending the correct usage of nails is paramount. Remember, the depth of the nail is critical. Nail heads shouldn't penetrate more than 1/8 inch into the wood. If they exceed this by 20% or more, supplemental nails are necessary. Moreover, to avoid fracturing, nails should be at least 3/8 inch away from the wood's edge and spaced at six-inch intervals.

The Significance of Shear Walls

Shear walls, often termed braced wall panels, are pivotal in areas with a high risk of seismic activities, like California. These walls are specifically designed to counter the sheer force exerted by lateral pressures, whether from earthquakes, wind, or the building's weight. A well-braced wall ensures that the load is uniformly distributed, lightening the burden on individual walls. The overall strength of a shear wall is a sum of its parts: the sheathing fasteners, framing members, and hold downs. Thus, it's essential to meticulously design and construct shear walls with the correct materials and proportions.

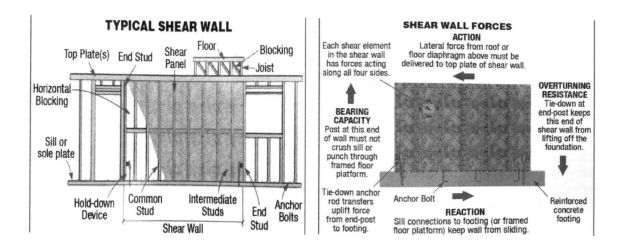

Guidelines for Constructing Floor Joists, Girders, and Posts

In certain conditions, the use of pressure-treated wood becomes essential. For example, wooden deck boards or patio construction that comes into direct contact with the ground should use this type of wood to prevent decay and insect damage. Similarly, wooden fence posts that are embedded into the ground should also be pressure-treated. A critical guideline to remember is that the base of posts supporting these structures needs to be elevated at least six inches from the ground unless they've undergone pressure treatment.

Deck Construction Essentials

In deck building, the utilization of pressure-treated or other durable lumber is non-negotiable. These decks, anchored securely for earthquake resilience, should be affixed to an adjoining exterior wall. If a deck stretches beyond 6 ft from the closest braced wall line, its design should be meticulously engineered using concrete.

Preserving Joist Integrity

While notching joists, a vital rule of thumb is to limit the notch depth to one-quarter of the joist's depth. Should there be a need to bore holes in the joists, these holes should never be within two inches of the joist's top or bottom, and their size shouldn't exceed one-third of the joist's depth.

Understanding Ledger Boards and Band Joists

A ledger board is attached directly to the house to support the joists for decks or extensions. The band joist, or rim joist, is the outermost joist in floor framing and is often responsible for transferring the weight or load from the ledger board to the underlying structure. It's essential to ensure proper installation and support mechanisms to prevent undue stress on the foundation or wall system.

Securing the Deck for Lateral Load Transfer

To safeguard against lateral loads, hold down tension devices, boasting a design capacity of at least 1500 pounds, should be set up at a minimum of two separate points on the deck. These apparatuses connect the deck's joist to the interior floor joist.

Wood Types and Span Capacities

Various woods like Southern Pine, Douglas Fir Larch, and Hem Fir are commonly used. The distance or span a joist can support varies based on its size and spacing:

- A two by eight joist spaced at 16 inches supports up to an 11-foot span.

- A two by 10 reaches up to a 14-foot span.

- A two by 12 can manage up to a 16-foot span when spaced at 24 inches.

However, using Southern Pine can reduce these spans by 2 feet when double beams are required. Douglas Fir Larch and Hem Fir demand larger dimensions for equivalent results.

For Southern Pine beams:

- A 22 by 6 supports up to a 5-foot span.

- A 22 by 8 can span up to 6 feet 6 inches.

- A 22 by 10 offers up to 8 feet.

- A 22 by 12 ensures up to 9 feet of span.

Stairway and Landing Specifications

Private stairways should have a minimum width of 36 inches. Any added trim and handrails shouldn't encroach more than 4.5 inches into this space. Steps should have a rise between 4 to 7.75 inches and a run of at least 10 inches. In the absence of nosing, treads should be at least 11 inches deep. Variations in tread width or riser height shouldn't exceed 3/8 of an inch in any stair flight.

Nosing, if provided on stairways with solid risers, should be between 0.75 to 1.25 inches. Open risers can be used in homes as long as a 4-inch sphere can't pass through.

The headroom of stairways must be at least 6 feet 8 inches. Space beneath stairs needs a one-hour fire-rated enclosure.

Landing specifications state that main external doors should have an adjacent landing that matches the door's width and is at least 36 inches deep. The height difference between the landing and the interior floor should not exceed 7.75 inches.

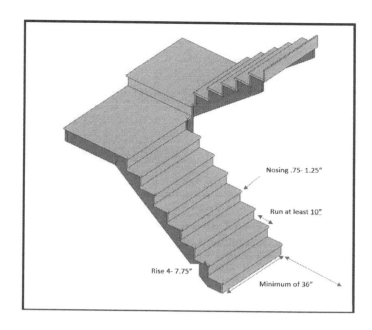

Handrails and Guardrails: Safety First

Handrails, crucial for stairway safety, should be present on one side if there are over four risers. The distance between a protruding handrail and a wall should be a minimum of 1.5 inches. These rails should sit 34 to 38 inches above stair treads and have smooth, graspable, and safe designs.

Guardrails, designed to prevent accidental falls, are mandatory on open sides of structures elevated more than 30 inches from the ground. They should stand at least 42 inches tall and be constructed so that openings prevent a 4-inch sphere from passing through. Additional guidelines ensure safety for various stairway configurations.

Roofing Essentials

Every building or home has a roof, making roofing knowledge essential for a general contractor preparing for the CSLB contractors license exam. This chapter will cover the common types of roofs, the basics of roof framing, and how to estimate roofing materials.

Roofs serve the primary purpose of protecting the building from weather conditions while requiring minimal maintenance. This means the roof must be able to withstand wind and snow loads. However, the style of the roof is also chosen for aesthetic appeal. As a contractor, you must be proficient in framing various types of roofs. The most common roof styles for homes are gable, hip, flat, and shed.

A gable roof, the most common type for homes, has two sloping sides that meet at the top, forming a gable at both ends. A gable is a triangular wall covered by the roof. A hip roof, on the other hand, has sloping sides all around the building. Unlike gable roofing, there is no gable, meaning this roof requires less maintenance and is stronger, making it suitable for regions with severe storms.

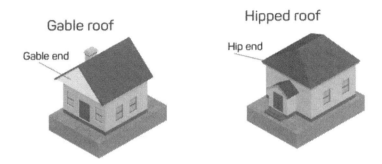

A shed roof, also known as a lean-to roof, slopes in one direction only and is often used as an addition to an existing structure. The roof may be attached to the side of the structure or to the roof. A gambrel roof is a symmetrical two-sided roof with two slopes on each side. The upper slope is positioned at a shallow angle, while the lower slope is steep. This design maximizes headroom inside the building's upper level and shortens what would otherwise be a tall roof.

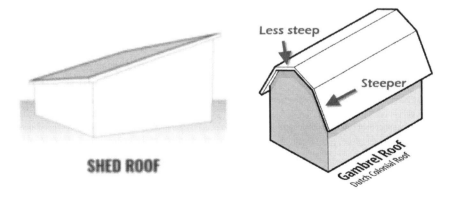

A low-slope roof, sometimes called a flat roof, is not perfectly flat. The rafters are inclined to form a slope to allow water to drain. The slope of a roof is determined by drainage design, attic volume, and roof pricing. Regulations establish 8/12 as the maximum workable slope. Extremely high slopes may require additional fasteners. Slopes of 1/12 or 2/12 are considered flat roofs and are not desirable due to leakage, ventilation, and ergonomic problems. The term "steep roof" is not universally defined and varies among contractors. Generally, a 4/12 slope up to 21/12 requires the use of steep-sloped materials for sheathing.

For roofs of 21/12, often called mansard roofing, additional fastening methods will be required. Steep roofs offer benefits such as durability of sheathing material, increased attic volume, attractive design, and easy water drainage.

For the state exam, you need to understand the basics of roof framing members. This information will be useful for general and estimating questions. The ridge boards are the elements receiving rafters from both sides of the roof's slope. They should be at least one inch thick and have a depth adequate for the rafters to be attached, plus two inches. Rafters must be attached by a gusset plate to the ridge board; direct nailing is not allowed. When perpendicular roof framing meets, a valley is created, leading to a hip. Valleys are when the corner direction goes inward, pointing towards the house, and hips are the opposite. When a valley or hip occurs, a valley or hip rafter is needed. This is a rafter from the corner to the ridge board. It must have a minimum thickness of two inches and a proper depth to accommodate the cut end of the rafters.

Due to the high load that valley rafters experience, they are usually doubled for a common house layout. A 2-inch by 10-inch or 3-inch by 8-inch should be sufficient, and a double rafter implementation is not needed, although it provides more room for nailing in that tricky section. Rafters are usually 2 by 8-inch members but can range from 2 inches by 4 inches to 2 inches by 12 inches. The slope of the roof and the rafter spacing are the main factors in determining the dimensions, as they control the span of the roof.

When a valley or hip is present, the rafters are called jack rafters and are provided to connect both ridge boards in valleys or the hip rafter to the exterior wall. Purlins can be implemented to reduce rafter spans so that smaller elements can be used as rafters in large spans. These purlins must have the same dimensions as the rafters they support. They must be continuous from start to end and should be braced with 2-inch by 4-inch braces, installed at 4 feet on center to an adjacent interior load-bearing wall at a minimum angle of 45 degrees from the horizontal surface. Braces must be 4 inches by 4 inches for lengths over 6 feet and spaced at 4 feet on center. However, these braces cannot be longer than 8 feet.

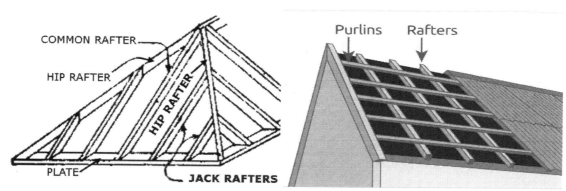

Another common member of the roof framing is the ceiling joist, also known as a rafter tie. These joists are commonly 2 inches by 6 inches, 2 inches by 8 inches, or 2 inches by 10 inches. Ceiling joists or rafter ties should be placed at the same location where rafters meet with the partition walls and should be properly secured to the walls and to the rafters' end with 16d common nails. These joists must be continuous from one end to the other and properly secured when they meet with interior load-bearing walls. The ends of ceiling joists can either be butted to the exterior walls or can be lapped a minimum of three inches using the toe-nailing technique to attach them.

In cases where ceiling joists cannot be connected to the rafters at the wall intersecting point, joists should be placed higher in the roof framing, acting as rafter ties. If the span between bearing walls is less than 25 feet, then engineering is not required. Finally, when joists are perpendicular to the rafters, rafter ties with a minimum dimension of 2 inches by 4 inches need to be placed with their proper metal connection.

The last common member in roof framing is the collar ties. These members are placed when high wind uplift forces are expected. They should have a minimum nominal dimension of 1 inch by 4 inches, spaced at no more than 4 feet on center, and placed in the upper third of the roof framing.

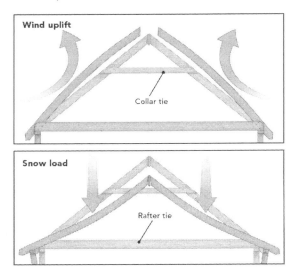

Notching, cutting, and drilling requirements for rafters are as follows: notches should not be greater than 16% or 1/6 of the rafter depth and should not be longer than a third of the rafter depth. They also cannot be located in the middle third of the span. In terms of holes, their diameter cannot be bigger than a third of the rafter depth and must be spaced at least two inches from both the bottom and top of the member and from an adjacent notch. A common notch made on the rafters is called a bird's mouth, which is a triangular notch made on the bottom of the rafters to achieve a high bearing value between rafters and walls. To create a bird's mouth, a horizontal cut called a seat cut must be made of the same length as the wall plate width, and a vertical cut called a heel cut of a maximum 1/6 the rafter depth.

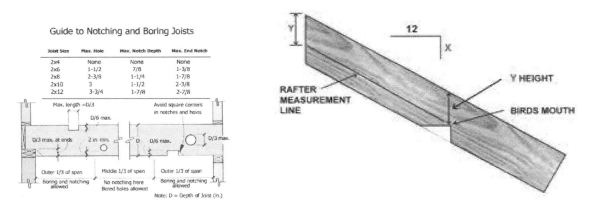

Ventilation plays a pivotal role in roofing, ensuring optimal temperature and moisture regulation within attic spaces. This not only prevents potential harm to the roof and the structure's interiors but also augments the lifespan of the roof, contributing to a building's energy efficiency. Specifically:

1. **Importance of Ventilation**: Proper roof ventilation thwarts condensation during colder periods and facilitates the escape of heat in warmer climates. Ventilation openings should range in size from a

minimum of 1/16 of an inch to a maximum of a quarter inch. Protecting these areas from environmental elements like corrosion is vital.

2. **Sizing and Placement**: Ventilation openings should equate to 1/150th of the net roof area—translating to one square foot of opening for every 150 square feet of the roof. Under specific circumstances, such as when vapor retarders or ventilators are in place, this ratio can be halved to 1/300th. For gable roofs, a singular louvered ventilation opening that aligns with the 1/150th guideline is commonly used. In contrast, hip roofs often feature slots at eave soffits paired with ventilators for ample air circulation. If eave vents are utilized, it's crucial to position insulation so as not to hinder airflow, maintaining a minimum of one inch of space between the roof sheathing and the insulation. The California Building Code provides guidance on conditions for unvented roofs or attics.

3. **Roof Framing Connectors**: Roof framing involves specific connectors, such as:

   - **Rafter to Ridge Board Connector**: This consists of a slim plate situated above the ridge, welded to a broader perpendicular plate that buttresses the rafter.

   - **Variable Pitch Connector (VPA)**: It facilitates the placement of rafters on the top wall plates, negating the need for a bird's mouth cut.

   - **Lateral Truss Rafter to Double Plate Connector**: This connector is favored in regions prone to high winds owing to its enhanced durability.

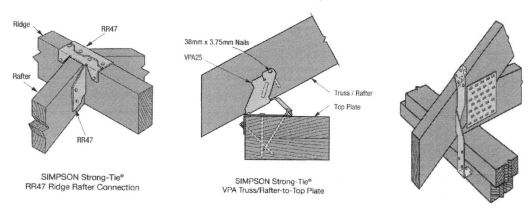

Rafter To Ridge Board   *Variable Pitch Connector*   *Lateral Truss Rafter to Double Plate Connector*

4. **Roofing Measurement Basics**: In the realm of roofing, a 'square' denotes 100 square feet (10 ft x 10 ft) of area. Material suppliers commonly price roofing materials by this metric. As an illustration, for a roof spanning 1200 square feet, the calculation involves dividing the overall square footage by 100. Consequently, a 1200 square foot roof would necessitate 12 squares.

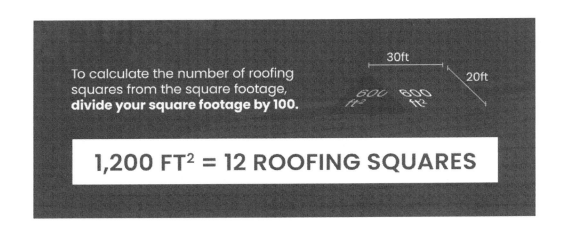

To calculate the number of roofing squares from the square footage, **divide your square footage by 100.**

30ft

20ft

600 ft² 600 ft²

1,200 FT² = 12 ROOFING SQUARES

Understanding Electrical Wiring: From Wire Types to Safety Measures
Wire Types and Their Specifications

When wiring a home, it's essential to understand the different wire types and their appropriate sizing. Wires can range from copper to aluminum, some suitable for outdoors while others are best for indoors. One prevalent kind of residential wiring is the Romex cable, an electrical conductor with a non-metallic sheathing. According to the National Electrical Code (NEC), Romex is categorized as either Underground Feeder (UF) or Non-Metallic Sheathed Cable (NM and NMC). Among these, the NMC cable is designed for damp environments like basements, thanks to its nonconducting, flame-resistant, and moisture-resistant coating.

Romex cables, typically used for lighting and outlet circuits in homes, come with labels like 12/2 or 12/3. The initial number reflects the wire gauge, usually 10, 12, or 14, and the latter denotes the number of conductors. The wire gauge also signifies the Romex cable's amperage rating. For example, a 12-gauge Romex cable, often encased in a yellow jacket, is rated for 20 amps and is ideal for small kitchen appliances. Conversely, a 10-gauge cable, with an orange jacket, is suitable for large appliances like an electric dryer.

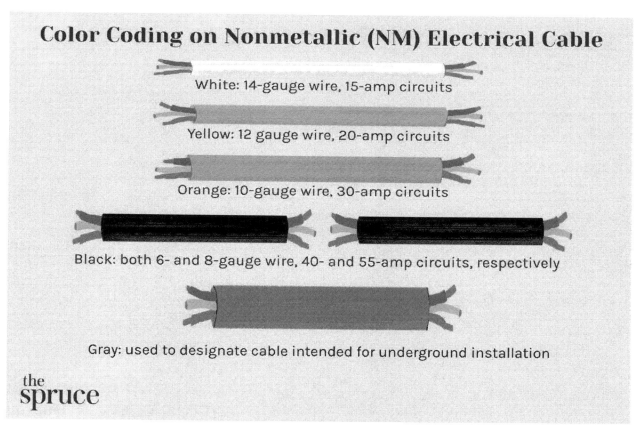

Color Coding on Nonmetallic (NM) Electrical Cable

White: 14-gauge wire, 15-amp circuits

Yellow: 12 gauge wire, 20-amp circuits

Orange: 10-gauge wire, 30-amp circuits

Black: both 6- and 8-gauge wire, 40- and 55-amp circuits, respectively

Gray: used to designate cable intended for underground installation

the spruce

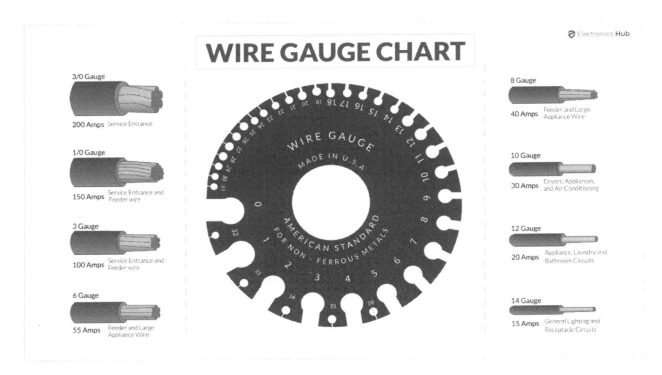

Setting Up the Electrical Service

The process of installing an electrical service commences with determining the appropriate size for the home. In the US, homes typically receive a 240-volt service from utilities, with two 120-volt lines and a neutral line. Modern homes often feature a 200-amp size electrical service. To curtail costs, the aluminum conductor, rather than copper, is the typical choice. The utility company not only decides the right size but also supplies the conductors and oversees their installation up to the house's electric meter.

For new electrical services, homeowners are responsible for laying out the conduit from the power source to the house's service point. However, the utility company handles conductor installation, electric meter setup, and security seal placements. Of the four wires supplying the main panel with power, three hail from the utility, and the fourth bare wire acts as the grounding conductor, ensuring that outlets connect to the ground. Proper understanding of these wire functions and connections is crucial.

Circuit Breakers and Safety Protocols

The chapter concludes with a focus on circuit breakers and fuses—essential components ensuring high-voltage residential wiring safety. Breakers, housed in the breaker box, come in various forms, such as single-pole breakers, double-pole breakers, GFCI breakers, and more.

Single-pole circuit breakers, common in homes, guard a single 120-volt circuit, usually rated at either 15 or 20 amps. In contrast, double-pole breakers protect 240-volt circuits used for heavy-duty appliances. Ground Fault Circuit Interrupter (GFCI) is another vital breaker type, especially relevant in damp environments. By measuring current discrepancies, GFCIs detect potential hazards, automatically tripping the circuit and reducing risks, making them indispensable in kitchens, bathrooms, and basements.

The Importance of GFCI Outlets

Ground Fault Circuit Interrupter (GFCI) outlets are vital in spaces like bathrooms and garages, where there's a high risk of coming into contact with water. These outlets, easily recognizable by their two vertical slots and a centered round hole, are designed to monitor the flow of electricity and prevent electrical shocks. If the GFCI detects an imbalance in the current flow, such as even a minor leak of four to five milliamps, it rapidly trips the circuit in less than 1/30 of a second.

However, users should be cautious: GFCI outlets aren't infallible. For instance, if you touch both the hot and neutral lines simultaneously, you could be shocked, and the GFCI might not detect it, leading to potential hazards.

For more extensive applications, like pools or hot tubs, multi-pole GFCI breakers become essential, albeit at a higher cost. When installing a GFCI outlet, given its bulky nature, consider using a larger box. And while one GFCI outlet can be installed on a conductor to protect further downstream outlets, it's typically recommended to have all outlets GFCI protected. Use provided stickers to identify and mark these protected outlets.

National Electric Code (NEC) on Electrical Wiring

The National Electric Code (NEC) sets forth guidelines for electrical wiring, ensuring safety across various contexts:

- **Kitchen Wiring:** A minimum of two 20-amp circuits are mandatory for portable appliances in kitchens and dining spaces, excluding lighting or permanently fixed appliances.

- **Bathroom Wiring:** Outlets should be installed within 3 feet of each basin. They can be on the cabinet side or face, provided they're under 12 inches from the countertop. However, outlets on the vanity countertop's surface or near tubs and showers are prohibited.

- **Outdoor Wiring:** Accessible receptacles are required at both the front and back of a dwelling, positioned no more than 6.5 feet above the ground level.

- **Light Switch Wiring:** Controlled lighting outlets are essential in all rooms, including bathrooms. If an interior staircase consists of six or more steps, switches at each entrance are obligatory.

Exterior Electrical Outlets and Lighting

It's necessary to have an outlet on the exterior side of grade-level doors and a lighting outlet at garage egress doors. Notably, garage vehicle doors don't require a separate lighting outlet.

The Importance of Grounding in Electrical Systems

Grounding the electrical system is pivotal for safety. It minimizes the risk of dangerous electric shocks which might happen when current leaks into the metal parts of electrical devices. In an effectively grounded system, this leakage, or fault current, is redirected safely away.

Most electrical systems come with fuses or circuit breakers to shield against severe fault currents. However, it's crucial to realize that currents under one ampere can fatally shock the human body, which is below what most breakers or fuses detect. Grounding acts as a protective measure against such incidents.

Yet, even with proper grounding, certain scenarios, like handling electronics on a wet surface, can pose fatal shock risks. To counteract this, safety devices called Ground Fault Circuit Interrupters (GFCI) are installed.

Home Grounding Practices

In many residences, the electrical system is grounded to an underground water supply system's metal pipe or a metal rod driven deep into the earth. This connection utilizes a copper conductor linking the pipe or rod to grounding terminals in the house's electrical panel.

Depending on the wiring system in use:

- Metal-sheathed electrical cable systems utilize the sheathing itself as the grounding mechanism between outlets and the service panel.

- Plastic-sheathed cable systems use an additional wire dedicated to grounding.

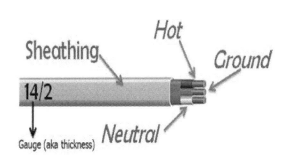

MC Cable, Sheath Listed as an
Equipment Grounding Conductor
330.108 Comment

Interlocked Type MC^AP® cable combines the metallic sheath with an uninsulated aluminum grounding/bonding conductor and is listed and identified as an equipment grounding conductor [250.118(10)b.].

Plastic Sheathed Romex with included insulated ground   *Metal Sheath as a Grounding Conductor*

Grounding and Appliances

Appliances intended for grounding come with a three-wire cord and a three-prong plug for connection to a corresponding outlet. This setup grounds the appliance's metal frame to the home's wiring system. Conversely, certain appliances with exposed heating components, like toasters, shouldn't be grounded due to increased shock risks. Double-insulated devices, built to ensure no external part becomes electrically live even with insulation failure, don't necessitate grounding.

Beyond Electrical Grounding: Lightning Protection

Grounding is also a crucial defense against lightning. Lightning rods and similar protective measures ground lightning strikes, safeguarding structures from potential harm.

HVAC Practices in California: Design, Placement, and Eco-Friendly Considerations

In California, HVAC (Heating, Ventilation, and Air Cooling) systems are a foundational aspect of residential construction. While they mostly align with nationwide trends in design and installation, the state's emphasis on environmental sustainability means advanced eco-friendly systems are available, but generally employed upon specific homeowner requests.

Furnace Placement and Specifications

The positioning of a furnace significantly influences the ductwork design. Typically, furnaces are situated in either the attic or the garage. While garage placement necessitates longer ducts, leading to marginally increased energy usage, the attic is the preferred location in California. This is in spite of the challenges presented by its elevated placement, such as the need for winches during installation. Crucially, furnaces should maintain a minimum gap of three inches for servicing or removal, and at least 24 inches should separate the attic entrance from the furnace's servicing platform.

Register Placement and Selection

Register placement follows the zone control strategy decided by the contractor. Common configurations include:

- Over windows or exterior walls: Two-way registers are optimal.

- Near interior walls: Either a one-way or three-way register, primarily directing towards an exterior wall or window.

- In the room's center: A four-way register, while considering the room's aesthetics and lighting arrangements.

Duct Design and Installation

Ducts, typically crafted from sheet metal, should maintain a minimum of a four-inch gap from the floor. Those embedded within concrete slabs require a minimum two-inch concrete encasement. While rectangular ducts need sturdy support on both sides, round ducts should not surpass a 40-inch diameter and need a snug fit. Direct 90-degree connections of ducts to registers are inadvisable; a transition fitter, like a rectangular box, is preferable.

Sizing AC Equipment

Calculating the area of rooms guides the AC equipment size. A single HVAC system is standard for double-story homes in California, emphasizing the need for impeccable design and leakage control. Generally, a three-ton AC unit delivers a cooling capacity of 36,000 BTU per hour, where one ton equals 12,000 BTU per hour.

Furnace Sizing

When determining furnace size, contractors rely on intricate load calculations. A simplified guideline suggests opting for furnaces generating 20 BTUs for every square foot. Hence, a home measuring 2,500 square feet would need a furnace producing 50,000 BTUs.

Refrigerants: Usage and Safety

Refrigerants, frequently chemicals with health and flammability concerns, demand stringent oversight. The building code stipulates permissible refrigerant quantities based on system type and room dimensions. Older air conditioning systems predominantly used R-22. However, the Clean Air Act bars its release during service, installation, or decommissioning. Modern systems adopt R-410A in place of R-22. While existing R-22 units can still be serviced with the same refrigerant without any EPA mandate to convert, retrofitting is permissible with approved alternatives. Among these, R-407C is retrofit-eligible, but R-410A isn't due to its elevated operational pressures.

Plumbing Guidelines: Regulations and Standard Practices

This chapter provides insights into the plumbing standards and regulatory framework in California. It encompasses potable water supply, waste venting, gas supply, and specific equipment regulations such as those for water heaters.

Key Water Properties

- Boiling Point: 212°F

- Freezing Point: 32°F

- Weight: One cubic foot of water weighs 62.4 lbs.; one gallon weighs 8.34 lbs.

- Volume: One cubic foot equals 7.48 gallons.

- Pressure: A water column height of 3.3 ft corresponds to 1.4 psi.

Pipe Support Regulations

The plumbing guide provides a table illustrating the requisite distances between horizontal supports. For instance:

- Plastic pipes: Supported every 4 ft.

- Copper pipes (2 inches or larger): Supported every 10 ft.

- Note: Direct contact with metal supports can result in noise during water flow, hence they shouldn't directly touch copper pipes.

- Gas pipes need more frequent support compared to water pipes.

- Underground pipes must be supported prior to backfilling. In uneven terrains, sand is used for leveling.

General Guidelines for Horizontal Support Spacing (in feet)

Nom. Pipe Size (in.)	SDR 21 PR200 & SDR 26 PR160					Schedule 40					Schedule 80					ABS PIPE Schedule 40				
	60	80	100	120	140	60	80	100	120	140	60	80	100	120	140	60	80	100	120	140
½	3½	3½	3	2		4½	4½	4	2½	2½	5	4½	4½	3	2½					
¾	4	3½	3	2		5	4½	4	2½	2½	5½	5	4½	3	2½					
1	4	4	3½	2		5½	5	4½	3	2½	6	5½	5	3½	3					
1¼	4	4	3½	2½		5½	5½	5	3	3	6	6	5½	3½	3					
1½	4½	4	4	2½		6	5½	5	3½	3	6½	6	5½	3½	3½	6	6	5½	3½	3
2	4½	4	4	3		6	5½	5	3½	3	7	6½	6	4	3½	6	6	5½	3½	3
2½	5	5	4½	3		7	6½	6	4	3½	7½	7½	6½	4½	4					
3	5½	5½	4½	3		7	7	6	4	3½	8	7½	7	4½	4	7	7	7	4	3½
4	6	5½	5	3½		7½	7	6½	4½	4	9	8½	7½	5	4½	7½	7½	7	4½	4
6	6½	6½	5½	4		8½	8	7½	5	4½	10	9½	9	6	5	8½	8½	8	5	4½
8	7	6½	6	5		9	8½	8	5	4½	11	10½	9½	6½	5½					
10						10	9	8½	5½	5	12	11	10	7	6					
12						11½	10½	9½	6½	5½	13	12	10½	7½	6½					
14						12	11	10	7	6	13½	13	11	8	7					
16						12½	11½	10½	7½	6½	14	13½	11½	8½	7½					

Water Supply Standards

- All plumbing fixtures require an uninterrupted supply of potable water.

- Potable water pipes: Identified by green bands with white letters.

- Non-potable water: Yellow bands with black uppercase letters stating "Caution, non-potable water do not drink."

Sizing the Water Supply Pipe

- Minimum size: Three-quarters of an inch.

- Many residences might need one-inch or larger pipes, based on the water demand.

- Consult the guide for detailed sizing information.

Backflow Prevention

Every plumbing setup needs a suitable backflow prevention device to avert pollution risks. Common systems include air gaps, AVBs, double-check valves, and barometric loops.

Water Supply Valves

- Valves up to two inches: Brass.

- Valves over two inches: Brass or cast iron.

- Every building and water heater should have a full-bore shut-off valve.

Pressure Requirements

- Minimum Pressure: 15 psi.

- If water pressure exceeds 80 psi, install a pressure regulator.

- Pressure relief valves must be automatic with drainage and set to 150 psi or below.

- Pressure regulators should be above-ground and weather-protected.

Water Supply System Testing

- Post-installation, test systems under water pressure no less than the operational pressure.

- Testing should ensure no leaks for a minimum of 15 minutes.

- Air pressure tests (50 psi) are an alternative to water tests, except for plastic piping.

Plumbing Fixture Standards

- Water closets should maintain a 15-inch minimum distance from side walls.

- There must be a 24-inch clearance in front of the fixture.

- Shower design should have a specific slope and dam dimensions.

Sanitary Drainage

Every water-utilizing fixture creates waste, managed by the sanitary piping system. Predominantly, PVC is used for sanitary piping. Other acceptable materials include cast iron, galvanized steel, copper, and certain grades of stainless steel. However, there are exceptions, detailed in the guide.

Drainage Slope and Sizing

- The recommended slope is one-quarter inch per foot.

- If this slope is unattainable, a larger pipe with a slope of 1/8 inch per foot can be used.

- Proper sizing is vital. For example, 20 fixture units necessitate a 3-inch drainage pipe.

Clean Outs: Every drainage pipe should have a cleanout located at its higher end, though certain exceptions exist. Cleanouts are necessary for every 100 ft and for combined directional changes exceeding 135 degrees. These cleanouts must be easily accessible and located near doors or crawl spaces for underfloor systems. To provide ease of access, there are specific size and clearance requirements, which also apply differently based on the cleanout's size. For underground systems, cleanouts should reach the grade level.

Traps and Venting: Traps should be installed as close to a fixture outlet as possible, ideally within 24 inches. Venting should be strategically placed near the trap, and specific criteria apply to ensure effective performance. Vents are typically made from PVC or copper, with sizing determined by the system's requirements. There are strict guidelines on how vent pipes integrate with drainage systems, and their exit points from buildings must adhere to specific height and distance rules to ensure safety and functionality.

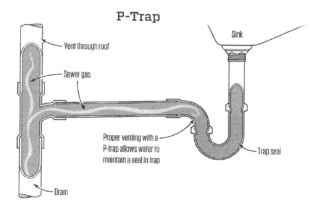

P-Trap

Testing of DWV Systems: After installation, drainage waste venting (DWV) systems should undergo thorough testing using either air or water to guarantee their integrity and proper function.

Water Heaters in Residential Settings: In California, water heaters usually find their place in garages. There are specific height requirements for burners and ignition devices to ensure safety. All installations or repairs require prior approval. Important components, like pressure and temperature limiting devices, must accompany all heaters. Additionally, in earthquake-prone California, seismic protection, like strategic strapping, is vital for all heaters.

Gas Piping: The effectiveness and safety of gas piping depend on the specific demands of the dwelling and the pressure requirements of appliances. Typically, gas piping is made from either plastic or metal, with plastic being the more prevalent choice. The durability of gas piping is paramount, often necessitating entire part replacements over mere repairs. Installation criteria for gas piping involve depth requirements for underground systems, protective measures when passing through walls, and specifics about orientation and pressure levels. The placement of gas outlets is also regulated to ensure safe access and use.

Residential Window Installation: Safety and Construction Standards

General Installation Considerations: Installing windows correctly is pivotal in construction, and adherence to the manufacturer's guidelines, including for new flashing windows, is essential. Windows in bedrooms have a distinct set of requirements to ensure they can serve as emergency exits. They must have an opening of at least 5.7 square feet, with a slight allowance to five square feet for windows at floor level. These windows need to be a minimum of 20 inches in width and 24 inches in height when opened fully. Additionally, the base of the window's opening should be positioned no more than 44 inches from the floor.

Pane Requirements in New Residences: Modern residential structures typically incorporate dual or double pane windows. These are mandatory for windows positioned 18 inches or less from the floor or situated near doors. If these conditions aren't met, both dual and single pane windows are acceptable.

Room-specific Window Criteria: The size of windows in habitable spaces is governed by specific standards. The glazed portion of the window must constitute at least 8% of a room's total floor area. Ventilation is another key aspect, with the window needing to open to at least 4% of the room's floor size. For example, in a 200-square-foot room, the window should cover at least 16 square feet, with the ability to open up to eight square feet for proper ventilation. Bathrooms have their own set of rules. They require a window opening of a minimum of three square feet, with at least half of it being operable. The need for a glazed area is eliminated if there's artificial lighting and a mechanical ventilation system in place.

Emergency Exit Windows: Safety remains paramount with the incorporation of emergency exit windows or doors in basements and bedrooms up to the third floor. These emergency exits should lead outdoors and must operate without needing any tools. While rooms can have supplementary smaller windows, only the larger ones qualify as exit openings.

Egress Window Requirements

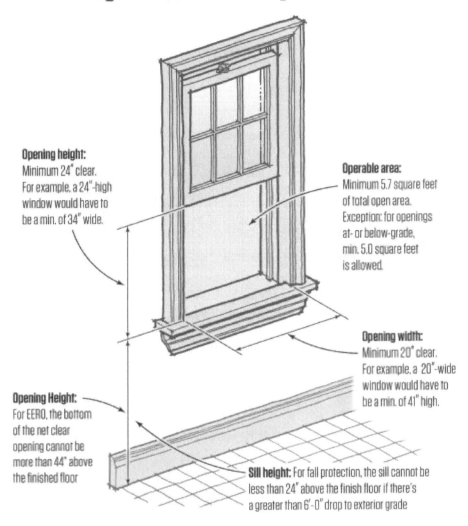

Opening height:
Minimum 24" clear.
For example, a 24"-high window would have to be a min. of 34" wide.

Operable area:
Minimum 5.7 square feet of total open area. Exception: for openings at- or below-grade, min. 5.0 square feet is allowed.

Opening width:
Minimum 20" clear.
For example, a 20"-wide window would have to be a min. of 41" high.

Opening Height:
For EERO, the bottom of the net clear opening cannot be more than 44" above the finished floor

Sill height: For fall protection, the sill cannot be less than 24" above the finish floor if there's a greater than 6'-0" drop to exterior grade

Lastly, emergency exit windows have stringent size regulations. They should provide a clear open area of at least 5.7 square feet, with height and width dimensions of 24 inches and 20 inches, respectively. If windows are designed for escape, their sill height should not exceed 44 inches from the floor, considering the clear opening and not the windowsill. For windows at ground level, a five-square-foot clear opening suffices.

Drywall Installation

Drywall, often referred to as sheet rock, gypsum board, wallboard, or plasterboard, is a widely-used material in the construction of walls and ceilings. Its success is attributed to its straightforward installation, repairability, and its aptitude to form smooth surfaces. Essentially, it comprises compressed rock enveloped in a paper covering.

Installation Pre-requisites: Before initiating the drywall installation, it's essential to ascertain that the building's exterior is sufficiently safeguarded against the weather and has cleared a preliminary inspection. It's recommended to start with the ceilings and then move to the walls. Sheets should align with one another without being forcibly pushed. Gaps between sheets shouldn't be wider than one-quarter inch, ensuring tapered edges lie adjacent.

Cutouts and Repairs: For elements like electrical outlets or fixtures, precise cutouts must be made, ensuring a clearance of no more than 1/8 inch. Any gaps wider than a quarter-inch necessitate patching using a joint compound and drywall tape.

Nailing and Fastening: While nailing, the nail head should rest in a slight dimple without damaging the board. Nails ought to be positioned 3/8 inch from board edges, with nails on adjoining edges aligning opposite one another. With a nailing system, maintain a seven-inch spacing for ceilings and eight-inch for walls. Alternatively, approved screws can be used, ensuring they're situated 3/8 inch from the board's extremities, and spaced 12 inches apart. Special attention: screws are mandatory for pocket door areas.

- For 1/2 inch drywall: Use 1-3/8 inch nails or 1-1/8 inch screws.
- For 5/8 inch drywall: Opt for 1.5 inch nails or 1-1/4 inch screws.

Reinforced corners should be flush with the wallboard, nailed roughly 12 inches apart. For edge metal trims, nail every six inches. If employing paperback corner bead, abide by the manufacturer's guidelines.

Material Considerations: For areas vulnerable to direct water exposure, like showers, or high moisture regions like saunas, the use of Greenboard is discouraged. Preferably, choose cement fiber, cement, or glass mat gypsum backers as foundational material for wall tiles in such spaces.

Fire-resistant Construction: Certain residential spaces demand a one-hour fire-resistance, notably walls separating attached garages from homes or enclosed spaces beneath staircases. A typical firewall is fashioned from type X gypsum wallboard, fastened at intervals of seven inches to 16-inch-spaced studs. All breaches and gaps should be taped or sealed with fire-resistant caulk.

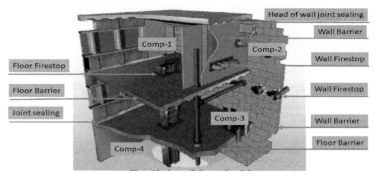

FIRECOMPARTMENTS IN A BUILDING

A Guide to Insulation Types and Their Applications

Insulation is essential for maintaining a consistent indoor temperature, enhancing comfort, and reducing energy costs. By acting as a protective layer against external weather conditions, it ensures energy efficiency.

Different Types of Insulation:

1. **Fiberglass Insulation:** Commonly used in walls, floors, and ceilings, it's available in bats, rolls, and can have a vapor barrier paper backing. When handling, use protective wear, as it can release particles causing respiratory or skin irritations.

2. **Cellulose Insulation:** Made from recycled paper, it's suitable for attics, walls, and spaces like between drywall. Despite being more effective than fiberglass, it can settle over time, diminishing its efficacy.

3. **Radiant Barrier Insulation:** Installed in attics, this insulation reflects heat, making homes cooler. For instance, Californian homes with this insulation tend to be 10 degrees cooler than those without it.

4. **Foam Insulation:** Typically used in new constructions, this cut-to-size foam panel enhances energy efficiency.

5. **Blown-In and Loose Fill Insulation:** These small foam and fiber particles are sprayed on walls, adhering tightly, making them perfect for insulating existing walls or hard-to-access places.

6. **Spray Foam Insulation:** Expanding upon application, it fills small spaces effectively and has a high R-value, which makes it apt for exterior walls.

7. **Fiberboard Insulation:** Thin yet high in R-value, it's best suited for air duct insulation or extremely hot climates.

8. **Radiant Barriers:** Primarily designed to reflect heat, they are perfect for hot summer attics. They should be paired with another insulation type in colder seasons.

Measuring Insulation Efficacy: The efficiency of insulation is determined by its R-value – a measure of its thermal resistance. Higher R-values signify superior insulation. For example, each inch of cellulose insulation has an R-value of approximately 3.5, which accumulates with thickness.

Local climate and building sections determine the required R-value. In central California, for instance, attics should have an R-value of at least 30, while walls should possess an R-value of 13.

Concept Check

1. What does Underground Service Alert assess?
   a) Soil stability
   b) Utility locations
   c) Drainage needs
   d) Permit requirements

2. When must you contact Underground Service Alert?
   a) During excavation
   b) After finding utilities
   c) 2-14 days before digging
   d) Only for major projects

3. What do white markings represent?
   a) Electric lines
   b) Proposed digging
   c) Chemical hazards
   d) Sewer lines

4. What ensures a level foundation surface?
   a) Grading
   b) Compacting
   c) Backfilling
   d) Excavating

5. What is a key grading reference point?
   a) Foundation outline
   b) Corner stakes
   c) Surveyor's transit
   d) Soil grade level

6. How are stakes elevated during grading?
   a) In 6 inch increments
   b) Based on soil type
   c) To match transit height
   d) By visual estimation

7. What is the first task when starting a construction project?
    a) Pouring concrete
    b) Setting rebar
    c) Placing forms
    d) Excavating footings

8. Where are the initial forms set?
    a) Around building perimeter
    b) In footing trenches
    c) On leveled ground
    d) Around columns

9. What determines footing depth below soil?
    a) Number of stories
    b) Soil type
    c) Rebar size
    d) Form materials

10. What does rebar reinforce?
    a) Formwork
    b) Foundations
    c) Concrete
    d) Walls

11. Where is rebar placed in stem walls?
    a) 4" from top
    b) 3" from top
    c) 2" from bottom
    d) 3" from bottom

12. How far should bottom rebar be from footing?
    a) 2-3 inches
    b) 3-4 inches
    c) 4-5 inches
    d) 5-6 inches

13. How often should anchor bolts be spaced for 2 stories?
    a) 4 feet
    b) 5 feet
    c) 6 feet
    d) 8 feet

14. How much rebar is needed for foundation electrode?
    a) 10 feet
    b) 15 feet
    c) 20 feet
    d) 25 feet

15. When is rich concrete mixture used?
    a) Mass concrete
    b) Waterproofing
    c) Reinforcing
    d) Foundations

16. What cement is used for most general uses?
    a) Type 1
    b) Type 2
    c) Type 3
    d) Type 4

17. What primarily affects concrete drying time?
    a) Admixtures
    b) Cement ratio
    c) Pour volume
    d) Weather

18. What concrete finishing step removes surface water?
    a) Troweling
    b) Leveling
    c) Bleeding
    d) Jointing

19. What is the smallest size nail commonly used?
    a) 2d
    b) 4d
    c) 6d
    d) 8d

20. What is required above doors and windows?
    a) Headers
    b) Cripples
    c) Jack studs
    d) King studs

21. What resists lateral force in shear walls?
    a) Siding
    b) Insulation
    c) Hold downs
    d) Drywall

22. When must floor joists use pressure-treated wood?
    a) Within 12 inches of ground
    b) Within 18 inches of ground
    c) Below concrete slab
    d) Above crawl space

23. What is the maximum notch depth in floor joists?
    a) 1/3 depth
    b) 1/4 depth
    c) 1/5 depth
    d) 1/6 depth

24. What is the minimum stair width per code?
    a) 32 inches
    b) 34 inches
    c) 36 inches
    d) 38 inches

25. Where must guardrails be installed?
    a) Decks
    b) Ramps
    c) Open sides over 30 inches high
    d) Around windows

26. What is the minimum handrail height from tread?
    a) 32 inches
    b) 34 inches
    c) 36 inches
    d) 38 inches

27. What connects rafters from both roof slopes?
    a) Purlins
    b) Joists
    c) Ridge board
    d) Valley

28. When is a valley rafter used?
    a) At roof peaks
    b) Where slopes join inward
    c) Under flat areas
    d) Along eaves

29. What attaches rafters to partition walls?
    a) Collar ties
    b) Purlins
    c) Ceiling joists
    d) Trusses

30. How should ceiling joist ends attach to walls?
    a) Direct nailing
    b) Toenailing
    c) Brackets
    d) Adhesive

31. What is the maximum rafter notch depth allowed?
    a) 1/4 of depth
    b) 1/3 of depth
    c) 1/5 of depth
    d) 1/6 of depth

32. What connector is used for variable rafter angles?
    a) Hip connector
    b) Ridge connector
    c) Variable pitch connector
    d) Eave connector

33. What type of Romex cable would be most suitable for wiring a basement?
    a) UF cable
    b) NM cable
    c) NMC cable
    d) 12-2 cable

34. What is the main purpose of a grounding conductor according to the National Electrical Code?
    a) To connect outlets to the electrical meter
    b) To connect the main panel to the ground
    c) To connect appliances to the utility lines
    d) To connect lighting circuits to the main panel

35. Which of the following conductors would typically be used for a new 200-amp residential service to help reduce costs?
    a) Copper
    b) Aluminum
    c) Silver-coated copper
    d) Gold-plated copper

36. What is the minimum number of 20-amp small appliance branch circuits required in kitchens per the NEC?
    a) 1
    b) 2
    c) 3
    d) 4

37. Which home grounding method utilizes a copper conductor to a metal water pipe?
    a) Concrete-encased electrode
    b) Ground ring
    c) Rod and pipe electrode
    d) Plate electrode

38. What type of appliance does NOT require grounding per NEC guidelines?
    a) Dishwasher
    b) Refrigerator
    c) Toaster
    d) Washing machine

39. What is the minimum clearance that should be maintained around a furnace installed in an attic per California building standards?
    a) 2 inches
    b) 12 inches
    c) 24 inches
    d) 36 inches

40. What method should be used to support underground water pipes prior to backfilling?
    a) Wire ties
    b) Hangers
    c) Sand
    d) Gravel

41. What color bands identify potable water pipes?
    a) Yellow
    b) Blue
    c) Green
    d) Red

42. What is the alternative to a water pressure test for checking new plumbing for leaks?
    a) Smoke test
    b) Dye test
    c) Air test
    d) Vacuum test

43. What should be installed if water pressure exceeds 80 psi?
    a) Expansion tank
    b) PRV
    c) Check valve
    d) Balancing valve

44. How far should plastic water pipes be horizontally supported apart?
    a) 2 feet
    b) 3 feet
    c) 4 feet
    d) 5 feet

45. What is the minimum slope required for drainage pipes when a 1/4 inch per foot slope cannot be achieved?
    a) 1/16 inch per foot
    b) 1/8 inch per foot
    c) 3/16 inch per foot
    d) 1/4 inch per foot

46. What seismic protection method helps secure water heaters?
    a) Bolting
    b) Strapping
    c) Shelf brackets
    d) Wall anchors

47. What is the maximum height allowed for a window sill if the window is intended for emergency escape?
    a) 42 inches
    b) 44 inches
    c) 46 inches
    d) 48 inches

48. What is the minimum operable area required for a bathroom window?
    a) 2 sq ft
    b) 2.5 sq ft
    c) 3 sq ft
    d) 4 sq ft

49. Where must dual pane windows be installed in new home construction?
    a) Living room
    b) Dining room
    c) Near exterior doors
    d) Kitchen

50. What is the minimum width of a window opening that serves as an emergency exit?
    a) 18 inches
    b) 20 inches
    c) 22 inches
    d) 24 inches

51. What is the maximum clearance allowed around electrical boxes when cutting drywall?
    a) 1/16 inch
    b) 1/8 inch
    c) 3/16 inch
    d) 1/4 inch

52. What drywall thickness requires 1-1/2 inch nails for installation?
    a) 1/4 inch
    b) 1/2 inch
    c) 5/8 inch
    d) 3/4 inch

53. How often should reinforced corner beads be nailed during drywall installation?
    a) 6 inches
    b) 8 inches
    c) 12 inches
    d) 16 inches

54. What fire-resistance rating is required for garage separation walls in homes?
    a) 30 minutes
    b) 45 minutes
    c) 1 hour
    d) 2 hours

55. Which insulation type is commonly used in existing wall cavities?
    a) Batt insulation
    b) Blown-in insulation
    c) Rigid foam
    d) Spray foam

56. What measurement indicates an insulation's thermal resistance?
    a) Density
    b) Thickness
    c) R-value
    d) Permeability

57. Which insulation type is made up of small, loose particles?
    a) Rigid foam
    b) Fiberglass rolls
    c) Cellulose
    d) Loose fill

Concept Check Solutions

1. B) Utility locations. California's Underground Service Alert analyzes excavation plans to locate and mark underground utilities at the site, preventing damage during digging. They do not assess soil stability, drainage, or permits.

2. C) 2-14 days before digging. California law mandates contacting Underground Service Alert between 2 and 14 days prior to starting excavation to get utilities marked. During excavation, after finding utilities, and for select projects does not satisfy the mandatory advance notice window.

3. B) Proposed digging. White markings by Underground Service Alert denote the proposed excavation or digging area. Electric, chemicals, sewers have different color codes per the utility marking standards.

4. A) Grading. Grading ensures an even, sloped or flat surface across the construction area, providing the necessary stable base for laying the building foundation.

5. C) Surveyor's transit. The original transit height is the key reference point during grading. Stakes are elevated to match this level all around the site perimeter.

6. C) To match transit height. During grading, survey stakes are lifted to the same height as the surveyor's transit to create a flat, level foundation zone.

7. C) Placing forms. The first construction task is placing concrete forms, which shape and mold the foundation after initial excavation. Concrete, rebar, and footings come after the initial forms are set.

8. A) Around building perimeter. The initial concrete forms are installed around the full perimeter of the planned building to establish the outline. Footing trenches, leveled ground, and columns are secondary form locations.

9. A) Number of stories. Footing depth below soil is determined by the building height, extending deeper for multi-story structures. Soil, rebar, and forms do not dictate footing depth.

10. C) Concrete. Rebar reinforces concrete, increasing its tensile strength, ductility, and resistance to cracking from applied loads and forces. It does not reinforce formwork, foundations, or walls.

11. B) 3" from top. For concrete stem walls under CRC, one #4 rebar should be within 12" of the top and 3" from the top of the footing. Not 2", 4", or at the bottom.

12. B) 3-4 inches. In stem wall and footing construction, bottom rebar should be 3-4 inches from the bottom of the footing per code.

13. A) 4 feet. For seismic design category E, anchor bolts on a 2-story building should be spaced at 4 feet on center according to the concrete construction diagram.

14. C) 20 feet. The foundation grounding electrode must have at least 20 feet of 1/2" rebar or copper conductor encased in concrete.

15. B) Waterproofing. Rich concrete mixtures are used for waterproof structures because of their high cement ratio.

16. A) Type 1. Type 1 Portland cement is formulated for general, normal usage in typical construction applications.

17. C) Pour volume. The most significant factor affecting concrete drying time is the volume or depth of the pour, as larger volumes take substantially longer to fully cure and harden. Cement ratio, weather, and admixtures have less impact.

18. C) Bleeding. Bleeding is the critical concrete finishing step where surface water rising up is allowed to evaporate naturally rather than being troweled back in, which can dilute and weaken the mixture.

19. A) 2d. The 2 penny or 2d nail, measuring 1 inch long, is the smallest common construction nail size used. 4d, 6d, and 8d designations are progressively larger.

20. A) Headers. Structural headers, typically doubled-up beams, must be installed over doors, windows, and other openings to provide sufficient support and transfer loads.

21. C) Hold downs. Special hold down connectors and fasteners are designed to resist the extreme lateral forces exerted on shear walls in seismic conditions.

22. B) Within 18 inches of ground. Wood floor joists or structural floors must use pressure-treated lumber if positioned within 18 inches of exposed ground per code. 12 inches, below slab, and above crawlspace don't dictate pressure treatment.

23. B) 1/4 depth. The maximum permissible notch depth when cutting notches in floor joists is 1/4 the joist's total depth. 1/3, 1/5, and 1/6 depths exceed the safe allowance.

24. C) 36 inches. The building code mandates a minimum stairway width of 36 inches in residential structures. 32, 34, and 38 inches violate the stair width requirements.

25. C) Open sides over 30 inches high. Guardrails are required by code on open sides of any walking surface elevated over 30 inches above the floor or grade below.

26. D) 38 inches. Handrails must be installed 34 to 38 inches above the stair treads as measured vertically from the nosing. Heights of 32, 34, and 36 inches are non-compliant.

27. C) Ridge board. A roof's ridge board is the critical framing member that rafters from opposite slopes get attached to, joining the two sides at the peak.

28. B) Where slopes join inward. A valley rafter is specially framed where two perpendicular roof slopes join together in an internal downward angle or valley.

29. C) Ceiling joists. Ceiling joists, or rafter ties, are used specifically to tie together and attach the rafter ends to the partition walls below.

30. B) Toenailing. Ceiling joist ends should be secured to walls using toenailing at an angle for optimal strength. Butting, direct nailing, brackets and adhesive are incorrect.

31. D) 1/6 of depth. Per code, the maximum rafter notch depth is limited to 1/6 or 16% of the total rafter depth. 1/4, 1/3, and 1/5 depths exceed the allowed notch size.

32. C) Variable pitch connector. A variable pitch connector allows attachment of rafters at varying angles to the wall top plates.

33. C) NMC cable. NMC cable has a moisture-resistant coating that makes it suitable for damp environments like basements. NM cable does not have this protective coating.

34. B) To connect the main panel to the ground. The grounding conductor connects the main electrical panel to the ground, providing a safe path for current in the event of a fault. This is a key safety requirement in the NEC.

35. B) Aluminum. Aluminum is typically used instead of more expensive copper for the conductors in a 200-amp residential service to help reduce installation costs without compromising safety and performance.

36. B) 2. The NEC mandates a minimum of two 20-amp small appliance branch circuits in kitchens and dining areas to provide sufficient power for common plug-in appliances. Only one circuit is insufficient per code.

37. C) Rod and pipe electrode. Connecting a copper grounding conductor between the electrical system and a metal water pipe is a common grounding method in many homes per NEC guidelines.

38. C) Toaster. Per the NEC, appliances like toasters with exposed heating elements should not be grounded due to increased electric shock risks if grounded.

39. C) 24 inches. California building standards mandate at least 24 inches of clearance around the furnace for servicing access. Less than this, such as 12 inches, is insufficient per code.

40. C) Sand. The plumbing code requires using sand to level and support underground water pipes prior to backfilling trenches. This ensures the pipes remain stable and avoids damage from uneven trench floors.

41. C) Green. Potable water pipes are identified by green bands with white lettering according to plumbing code labeling requirements. This differentiates drinking water lines from non-potable or waste lines.

42. C) Air test. A suitable alternative to a water pressure test for checking new plumbing systems is an air test pressurized to 50 psi, according to the plumbing code. However, this method cannot be used on plastic pipes.

43. B) PRV. If water pressure exceeds 80 psi, a pressure reducing valve (PRV) should be installed per code to regulate pressure down to safer levels. Other devices like check valves do not serve this purpose.

44. C) 4 feet. The plumbing code specifies that horizontal support is needed every 4 feet for plastic water supply pipes. More frequent support is required for materials like copper.

45. B) 1/8 inch per foot. When the standard 1/4 inch per foot drainage slope cannot be achieved, the plumbing code allows using a larger pipe with a reduced minimum slope of 1/8 inch per foot. Slopes less than this would not provide adequate drainage.

46. B) Strapping. Seismic strapping helps secure water heaters and prevent tipping during earthquakes. Bolting, brackets, or anchors alone do not provide adequate protection per code.

47. B) 44 inches. The maximum height allowed by code for a window sill serving as an emergency escape is 44 inches from the floor. Greater heights would impede egress.

48. C) 3 sq ft. Bathroom windows are required to have a minimum operable opening area of 3 square feet per code. This ensures adequate ventilation can be achieved when opened.

49. C) Near exterior doors. Dual pane windows must be installed near exterior doors in new homes to meet energy efficiency codes. Other locations can use single pane.

50. B) 20 inches. Emergency exit window openings must be at least 20 inches wide according to code minimums. Narrower widths than this would impede egress.

51. B) 1/8 inch. The maximum clearance permitted around electrical boxes when cutting drywall is 1/8 inch. Larger gaps require mud and tape repairs to avoid fire hazards.

52. C) 5/8 inch. Drywall sheets of 5/8 inch thickness require minimum 1-1/2 inch nails per manufacturer specifications and building standards. Thinner or thicker sheets need different fastener sizes.

53. C) 12 inches. Reinforced corner beads should be nailed every 12 inches during installation to provide adequate stability and angle support. More frequent nailing is often needed for trim beads.

54. C) 1 hour. A 1 hour fire resistance rating is mandated by code for walls separating garages from residential units. This is commonly achieved using type X gypsum wallboard.

55. B) Blown-in insulation. Blown-in insulation made of small particles is well-suited for installing into existing wall cavities. Batt and rigid foam insulations are more difficult to retrofit into closed wall spaces.

56. C) R-value. An insulation's R-value indicates its effectiveness in providing thermal resistance. Higher R-values represent better insulative performance and ability to resist conductive heat flow.

57. D) Loose fill. Loose fill insulation is composed of many tiny fiber or foam particles that are blown into spaces. This category of insulation has loose, granular particles rather than solid sheets or rigid boards.

Thank you for trusting us to be a part of your journey towards success. We're here to help you grow and achieve your goals, and your feedback is invaluable to us. As you reflect on your preparation journey, we kindly ask you to share your thoughts through a review. Your positive words can encourage others and help them feel confident in choosing the right test prep resource. We truly appreciate your insights and the time you take to help us improve. Thanks once again for choosing us, and here's to your continued success!

Made in the USA
Las Vegas, NV
04 March 2024

86679321R00109